Best wishes

(signature)

(signature)

A Listening Ear

MORE STORIES FROM THE HEART OF RURAL IRELAND

Michael Healy-Rae

Gill Books

Gill Books
Hume Avenue
Park West
Dublin 12
www.gillbooks.ie
Gill Books is an imprint of M.H. Gill and Co.

978 07171 8629 7

Designed by Carole Lynch
Edited by Tara King

Printed by ScandBook UAB, Lithuania

This book is typeset in Minion.

The paper used in this book comes from the wood pulp
of managed forests. For every tree felled, at least one tree
is planted, thereby renewing natural resources.

A CIP catalogue record for this book is available from
the British Library.

5 4 3 2 1

Dedicated to the great characters whose real-life stories and events make up the content of this book. I will always be eternally grateful for their friendship and support.

Life. Don't blink or you'll miss it.
— MHR

Introduction

It must have been said to me at least a hundred times inside in funeral homes, 'Do you know what we were doing this past week? We were reading stories to himself from your book, *Time to Talk*.'

Now bear in mind, the 'himself' they would be referring to (or 'herself', as the case often was) would be the person within in the coffin. I remember one night I went to a wake above in Dublin. An unusual occurrence, to say the least, as wakes are more of a country tradition, but the family in question had strong links to Kerry so I went in to pay my respects. As I was walking in, didn't I hear them telling a story about how, as the now-deceased man was dying, they had been reading stories to him from *Time to Talk*. The man was unconscious, but the family kept reading stories from the book as there was a lot of good humour and nostalgia in it, the kind that he would have loved. After about ten or twelve hours, there was no response from the man.

Later, as the family were sitting around the man's bed, chatting about all sorts, one of the family brought up a story from the book, the one about me having six grandmothers. As they were talking and laughing about it, someone said, 'Sure wasn't it five grandmothers he had, not six?'

Next thing didn't the dying man in the bed open his eyes and pipe up, 'You're wrong!' he said. ''Twas six!'

Well, whether you're in this world, or on your way to the next one, I hope this book provides as much enjoyment as the last one.

Michael Healy-Rae

A Listening Ear

Field Wise

It's my honestly held belief that people who live in very remote and rural areas have a strain of ingenious running through them. Sure they're the most resourceful breed of people you will ever meet. It's like 'streetwise', but without the streets, if you know what I mean. I'd love to call it 'fieldwise' but that doesn't pack nearly the same punch, unfortunately.

I remember once there was a family that lived way out in a far-flung corner of Kerry. This place was even further beyond the 'back of beyond'! Their house was situated up a long, rocky slope that could actually be quite difficult to scale at the best of times. While the brothers who lived there knew how to manoeuvre their own jeep up the slope to the house, the standard car definitely wouldn't manage it.

When their mother passed away, they were faced with a dilemma. How would they get the poor woman into the coffin when the hearse wouldn't be able to drive up the road to their house? Most people wouldn't know how to get around this, but straight away, the brothers knew exactly what to do. They got on the phone to the undertaker and told him that it was a matter of urgency that he meet them at a particular location with a coffin. The undertaker of course tried to reassure them that there was no rush and they could take some time with their mother if they wished, but they were adamant that he meet them, with a coffin in tow, at a specific location ASAP. The undertaker, despite being a person of great understanding, was awful confused by this instruction, because he knew the brothers and he knew that the house where their mother had passed away was a in a completely different location to where they wanted him to bring the coffin.

Despite his reservations, he did as they asked, and arrived as swiftly as he could with the coffin in the back of the hearse. The brothers were already there waiting for him. And who do you think they had with them? Their mother, in the passenger seat, no less. They knew that the hearse, being long and low, wouldn't have had a hope of being able to make it up the bad road to their house, so in order to get their mother into a coffin, they knew that they had to act quickly and find a solution before rigor mortis set in. The brothers had carried her out to the car, pushed back the passenger seat as far as they could, laid her back, and then secured her in place. All done as respectfully as possible, I hasten to add. Off she went in the hearse, disaster avoided. If ever there was a classic case of Kerry intelligence at work, well lads, I have to say it was definitely there.

Don't Wrong John

In rural Ireland, when someone is always one step ahead of the game, they'd usually be referred to as 'canny', 'wacky', 'cute', or 'sharp'. There's no fooling them, and mother of God, you'd have to be a fool to even try. One situation that springs to mind is that of a Kilgarvan man, John Lyne, who adopted a very smart approach after he realised he had been conned. John was a very good friend and neighbour of mine; a terribly generous, kind and considerate man who was also hugely respected and highly thought of in the community. As a result of his work as a farmer and cattle dealer, he was also a pretty tough man.

Well, one day a few years back, John sold a lorry of cattle to another cattle dealer from up the country. Now, John thought he knew this dealer well; he genuinely believed he was a decent, honourable individual, so when a cheque was produced for the purchase, he naturally didn't think anything of it. A couple of days later, John went into the bank to cash the cheque only to be told there was no money to honour the payment. The cheque had bounced, and John had no other option but to go home with the bloody thing still in his pocket and no money for the lorry load of fine cattle that he had sold in exchange for it.

All the way home, John was racking his brain thinking about what he could do to get the money he was owed. Most men would have picked up the phone and launched an all-merciful verbal attack. What John did, however, was the opposite. He kept his cool, maintained his nerve, and with a plan in mind, he calmly phoned the cattle dealer that had conned him. The man answered. There was no caller ID back then!

'Thanks be to God I got you,' said John, an air of relief evident in his voice.

Now the cattle dealer on the other end of the phone was no doubt expecting to get an earful, but this is what he got instead.

'I'm in an awful way and you're the only man who can help me. My mother is very sick and I'm afraid she won't do the next few days. There's a big shed of cattle at home and I have to get rid of them before anything happens to my mother. All I want you to do is take the cattle from me. Will you take them off my hands?'

The man, of course, was delighted by this proposition and said he would.

John, however, wasn't finished.

'There's a good few lorry loads of cattle there so when you're coming down, I'd say it would be a good idea to have a couple of lorries coming with you. I don't mind what day you come, but if you can, try to be here within the next few days so it's all sorted and finished should the worst happen to my mother. We won't even talk about money because I know you're an honourable man and an honest man. I won't even insult you by asking what you'll give me for them because I know you'll give me their value.'

John was coming across so genuine on the phone that the man was swallowing his story, hook, line, and sinker. As the conversation was nearing the end, John then put the tin hat on it altogether.

'By the way,' he said. 'With all that's going on at home with mother, I never got to go to the bank yet with the cheque you gave me the last day. If it's alright with you, I might go in with it in the next day or two because I might need a bit of money if we have a funeral to plan.'

The following morning, what did the cattle dealer do but head straight for the bank to lodge the funds so the first cheque would be cleared for John to cash. Sure enough, John got his money for the lorry load of cattle and off he went to prepare for the cattle dealer's arrival.

That very day, the cattle dealer headed for Kerry to collect these lorry loads of cattle from John. He was no doubt certain he would get double if not triple the number of cattle this time around. He was in for the big kill and arrived into the farmyard with massive lorries and trailers to carry the cattle. John emerged from the house holding a stick. The cattle dealer presumed he was getting ready to load the cattle with him, so he took no notice and hopped out of his lorry.

'Tell me, how's poor mother?' he asked, feigning interest.

By God, John wasn't having any of it. 'Mother? I'll give you mother, you thievin' blaggard!'

You can be sure there were a few more expletives thrown into the mix as John went and chased the cattle dealer back to his lorry. He escaped unscathed and injury-free, but you know, when it comes to an individual like that, well you wouldn't be sorry to see them get a belt or two. I thought John's approach to the problem was genius. No university will teach a person that type of canny skill. When it comes to real raw intelligence versus doing things by the book, well, I'll take the former over the latter any day.

To be honest, I will never understand businesspeople who employ conman's logic. I can't see why they think they're getting the better half of the deal by scamming someone for short-term gain, when if they were just honest and kept things above board, they would actually earn more in the long run and both sides would be happy. You'd often hear of the expression that such-and-such a person 'couldn't lie straight in the bed.' It was another way of saying they were crooked in their business dealings. I'm a firm believer that if you can't do a straight deal and are crooked, then you'll always be that way. People can change but I don't buy into the theory that a person of that nature can mend their ways.

I'll always remember an incident that occurred after a good friend of mine went to view a car in the hope of purchasing it. It looked great, had all the paperwork and requirements he wanted, so he decided to go ahead and buy it. When the payment was made and the car was delivered, he realised there was something a bit different about it. That's when it dawned on him that there had been four brand-new tyres on it during the viewing, but they had since been replaced with four bald tyres complete with cracked sidewalls. I knew both sides of this deal and I've kept an eye on the seller ever since. Not a euro will I put his way. Tricks? Those things won't take you anywhere in life.

Are Ye Looking for Work, Lads?

Sometimes bizarre things will happen, but on occasion the bizarre is just so bizarre that you know it couldn't have been made up. Two stories come to mind on this. The first one is about a very nice Kilgarvan man called Denis Lynch who was living and working in New York. One evening following work, Denis went into a pub for a pint where he struck up a conversation with two young British lads. Now, Denis was a very sociable man, one you would have the craic with and the kind who could even put talk on a monk during a vow of silence. These two young men were really taken with Denis and the more he chatted, the more they liked him. Every now and then, these other men would approach the two young lads and say something like, 'we have to be watching the clock, we need to get going,' but they were having such a good laugh with Denis, they would wave away these time-conscious men. Denis of course took no notice in the whole wide world.

When they eventually got up to leave, they asked Denis if he would come to the pub again the following evening as they would be there and would like to meet him for a pint again. Denis hummed and hawed a bit about it but said he'd try. That was fine. The following evening he was on his way home from work. He hadn't forgotten about the two lads, but with it being New York, he figured they would be out looking for work and not stuck in a bar waiting for him, so he didn't bother going in.

The following evening after that again, he went into the pub. The barman started pulling a pint for him.

'Oh my God, Denis,' he said. 'You left two lads awful disappointed yesterday evening. They had other people with them, and you know, they were all looking forward to meeting you.'

Now Denis had just come in from a long day at work; all he wanted was to have a pint in peace and he sure as hell wasn't in the form for a side of guilt with his Guinness.

'Well God damn it, sure what about them?' he said to the barman. 'C'mere, did they get some work, do you know? I'd say it was work they were looking for.'

The barman got into a fit of laughing.

'How do you mean, "did they get work", Denis?' he asked.

'Well they were two young lads and sure did you see the state of their trousers? Their arse was falling out of their back pockets. Were they over here looking to get work; to get the auld start like?'

The barman was dumbfounded.

'You really don't know who they were?'

'No, sure I never saw them before in my life!'

'You don't have a clue?'

'No. They were nice young lads, but sure what's the big deal about them?'

'Denis, those lads are the two Gallagher brothers, Liam and Noel. They're in the band Oasis!'

Oasis were in their prime at that stage; I'd say they were one of the biggest bands on the planet, so I think the reason they really took to Denis was because they knew that he genuinely didn't know the first thing in the world about them. He was having the craic with them and not asking for autographs and all that carry-on. He didn't give a tuppenny damn about them. All they were to him were two young scruffy British lads likely over in New York looking for work. As it happens, he had even told them that if they had trouble finding work, they could give him a shout and he would try to help. Denis knew as much about Oasis as a pig would know about a holiday, and I'd say even after he was told who they were, he still didn't give a tuppenny damn about them!

Now, let me tell you the second story that comes to mind, and lads, this is the best one altogether.

Two Yanks and One Slap Across the Hand

The Loo Bridge Bar, which is about eight miles outside of Kilgarvan, and was operated by a very nice man called Matt, was very nearly the scene of an awful catastrophe altogether. I mean the sort that could have made international headlines had disaster not been narrowly avoided. One day, a local character called Ger The Manny was sitting at the bar having a pint. I should point out here that Ger's actual surname was Donoghue but he had been given the nickname 'Ger The Manny' and so was always referred to as such. What it means or why he was given it, I honestly couldn't tell you.

Now Ger The Manny had a walking stick which he brought everywhere with him, but whenever he was sitting at the bar, he had a habit of putting the stick up on the counter beside his pint. While he was there this particular day, who should walk in but a young American couple – a dark-haired man and a beautiful red-haired lady. The woman took her seat while the man went to the bar and ordered two Diet Cokes, which, he specified, they wanted 'with lots of ice'. Matt gave the Yank the two drinks and had a bit of chit chat with him before heading off out the back to check something or other.

While Matt was gone, however, didn't the Yank lean in over the counter. As he was about to reach out to get something, Ger The Manny grabbed his walking stick and tried to land the Yank's hand with a ferocious belt. He just barely missed the hand by about an inch, I'd say.

Next thing didn't Ger The Manny start roaring. Now to give you an idea of what the Yank was seeing at this stage, try to picture an elderly enough man with a strong Kerry accent, angrily waving a walking stick and shouting, 'Go back, you blaggard!'

9

Matt, who was still out the back, had heard the commotion and came running out. 'Ger! Christ, what's wrong?' he asked.

'Ha! That so and so was leaning in over the counter trying to steal your fags,' said Ger, pointing the stick while practically frothing with temper.

The shocked Yank looked at him, put out his two hands and said, 'My goodness, I'm so sorry. All I was doing was leaning in to try and get a little bit more ice.'

'You were not, you blaggard!' insisted Ger The Manny. 'You were trying to steal poor Matt's fags!'

The Yank swore he was doing no such thing. Meanwhile, the woman who had walked in with him was still in her seat looking on, horrified by what was happening. There was no calming Ger The Manny, however, so they quickly finished up their drinks and left shortly after.

That night, a couple of locals arrived into the bar for a drink.

'Well, Matt,' they said. 'I suppose you won't be talking to us at all tonight!'

'Why wouldn't I?' asked Matt, bemused by such a remark.

'Well sure aren't you hanging around with the bigwigs now?'

'What in dear God are you talking about? Are ye raving?'

'The big shots! The ones you had in here earlier!' they explained.

'Sure I had no one in today only Ger The Manny, a couple of locals … ah God, there were two Yanks who called in as well! They the big shots you're on about?'

The local looked at him, a bit stunned. 'You really don't know, Matt? Did you not see the big black cars and all the men standing around the yard while the two were in here?'

'No! I saw nothing at all. Who were they?'

'Tom Cruise and Nicole Kidman, that's who!'

It turns out, Tom and Nicole were on their way to Kenmare when they decided to stop off in a quiet pub for two soft drinks.

They thought it would be a nice break in the journey when in fact
they weren't five minutes inside the door of the pub when poor
Tom nearly had the hand taken off him thanks to Ger The Manny
and his walking stick!

A Tom Gill Egg

I went to school with many a great character, but a young man called Thomas Gill definitely had more 'character' than most. Now Thomas was always a great student, not to mention a mighty hurler and footballer. He was a triple threat. Come the early-to-mid-1980s, however, and sure wasn't he tempted by the bright lights of America. He decided to swap the sliotars for the skyscrapers and head for New York. The only obstacle in his way was getting the visa to go. Now, Thomas's mother, Nelly Gill, would always have been very religious, but didn't the bit of religion rub off on Thomas. After he had filled out the application form for his visa, what did he do only head over to the church where there was a very important holy statue. Well, Thomas must have spent a good ten minutes if not more rubbing the application form on the statue for good luck before posting it off. Sure enough, God came through for him, got him the visa, and Ireland's loss was America's gain.

I can always tell when Thomas is home because I always hear him before I see him. He doesn't even need to tell me he's calling into the shop to see me; I'll hear his banter and laughter getting progressively louder the closer he gets to the door!

His father, Tom Gill, who has since gone to his eternal reward, used to come back to the shop every day and would spend hours keeping an eye on things for me. I gave him the nickname the Chief of Staff. At the time, Tom's wife Nelly used to mind our young lads and a very excellent job she did too. My youngest son, Kevin, adored Tom. Everything out of his mouth would be, 'Tom Gill did this', 'Tom Gill said that'. Kevin would never call Tom by just his first name either, he always referred to him as 'Tom Gill'.

When Tom would be shaving, Kevin would stand there watching

him. Now Tom would always shave the old-fashioned way with a razor blade, shaving foam and the sink full of grey sudsy water. Kevin, who was about four or five at the time, was fascinated by this. One day anyway didn't he decide to be like Tom Gill and down the stairs he came with shaving foam on his face.

'Nelly?' he said, 'I'm after shaving myself too, like Tom Gill.'

Of course Nelly laughed and took no notice until Kevin said, 'I shaved! Look!'

Whatever way she looked didn't she see that Kevin had very tastefully shaved off his eyebrow. He had managed to find a box to place in front of the bathroom sink so he could stand up on it to see himself in the mirror. He then found Tom's razor and shaving foam, plastered it on his eyebrow and shaved the whole thing off. There he was, proud as punch after having cut the eyebrow off himself. For good measure, hadn't he also taken some aftershave and splashed it on his face, 'just like Tom Gill'.

It was the same whenever Tom would be eating. Nelly was a seriously good cook, and each morning, Tom would have a breakfast fit for a king. One of the things he would always have was a boiled egg. The thing is, Tom also had a daily routine when it came to his boiled egg. He would crack open the egg with his spoon, take a small bit of butter and smear it over the top. He would then take a little salt and sprinkle it over it the butter, before mixing the two into the yolk to create that lovely creamy blend. Well, Kevin used to call that 'a Tom Gill egg'. It wasn't an egg, it wasn't a boiled egg, it was a Tom Gill egg.

When Thomas was living over in America, anyway, he would phone home on a regular basis. The gas thing is, sometimes he would be the one telling his mother Nelly the news from around Kerry. Back then, the equivalent of a smartphone was the bush telegraph, and it was a mighty network altogether. I'll tell you one thing, coverage and network congestion were never an issue.

I'll always remember the story of Nelly finding out news about a great man called John Reilly who lived in Reilly's bar. You could see Reilly's bar from Nelly's door. In fact, she was so close to it, she could have fired a stone without any effort and still hit Reilly's front door. One day, Nelly got a phone call from Thomas in New York.

'Isn't it awful sad about John Reilly?' said Thomas.

'What's wrong with John Reilly?' asked Nelly.

'Sure isn't he after dying?'

'Is he?'

'He is, I'm telling you!'

He was 3,000 miles away and Nelly not even 300 yards away and she had no idea. Sure who needed Facebook or mobiles when you had the Kilgarvan bush telegraph!

A Bad Enough Fright

There are certain stories you'd hear as a child, and you know, even as an adult, you'd be fully convinced there's some truth in them. I remember my father telling me a story about an incident that happened when he was working in Moll's Gap. He spent years and years in the Gap, driving a digger there and blasting rock. At one point, there was a man called Dan Breen from nearby Blackwater working alongside him. While my father was breaking and crushing stone at the top of Moll's Gap one day, Dan was working the tractor. As he was working, didn't poor Dan have an awful accident. He went off the edge of the road with the tractor and down a massive cliff face. Sure he was nearly killed. Of course, Dan was hospitalised, and people were awful worried about him. He was so bad I'd say the last rites were swiftly administered. He pulled through, thank God, but what shocked people most wasn't his recovery but his hair!

When Dan first went into hospital, he'd had a big head of black hair. The story goes that by the time Dan left hospital some weeks later, every hair on his head had gone from jet black to Tippex white. When I was young and growing up, we'd hear this story about Dan and be warned that if you got a bad enough fright your hair would completely change colour. In my case, I've had plenty of close shaves with death, plenty of accidents and certainly plenty of frights, but instead of my hair changing colour, didn't the damn thing just up and leave my head entirely!

Fire in the Trenches

In every parish, you'll have different types of people and different types of characters. Some are contrary auld so-and-sos, some are the complete opposite, and some are halfway in between, but when you take two hardcore supporters from different sides of the political spectrum and set them against each other, well, you have yourself a whole new breed of character entirely. I discovered this for myself a good few years back.

I was up on the machine digging a trench to lay a water pipe. Denis Healy, a local Fine Gael supporter, and a well-liked, hard-working man, was working alongside me, overseeing the job. One day, as we were working on the site, who should drive by only Tadgh Quill, a great supporter of Fianna Fáil. Now, Tadgh was a gentleman, a lifelong pioneer and a great character. Whenever Tadgh was driving, the window would always be rolled down and he'd be half leaning out while he smoked a cigarette. As I was on the digger, Tadgh drove past the site, waved in and shouted out some friendly salute like, 'Howye lads'. Denis was on the other side of the digger and hadn't seen Tadgh, he just saw the car as it was driving on. What you need to know here is that because of their political differences, Denis and Tadgh would never have been in the same political camp. Anyway, didn't Denis turn to me and ask, 'What did that man say?'

'Oh I don't want to repeat it at all,' I said.

Of course that only made Denis worse.

'Tell me what he said!'

'I won't,' I insisted. 'I don't want to be causing trouble.'

The truth of the matter is that Tadgh had said nothing, only saluted us.

After a desperate amount of persuasion, I eventually gave in to Denis. 'Alright! I'll tell you what he said, but don't blame me!'

'Well, what did he say so?' Poor Denis was nearly blue in the face at this point.

'What Tadgh shouted out the window was, "Eff off you auld Blueshirt!"'

Well, Denis was hopping with the anger; sparks were coming out of him with the height of temper.

'He said that?'

'He did!' I said.

'I'll get him. I'll get him yet,' Denis replied, absolutely fuming.

Well, that was all fine, but didn't I forget to set Denis straight and tell him I was only joking. We got distracted by the job and it went out of my head completely. A couple of days later, poor Tadgh was coming out of Quills' shop after getting the messages, and who was on his way in after parking his bicycle only Denis. The red mist descended and didn't Denis start rolling up his sleeves.

'Come on now, you Fianna Fáil blaggard, you say it to my face,' he shouted at Tadgh.

Poor Tadgh was stunned. 'Say what? Sure I never said anything!'

'Ha! I heard alright what you said!' said Denis back.

Next thing didn't the row start outside the shop between the two men. It got back to me later that day that World War III had broken out between Fine Gael and Fianna Fáil outside Quills' shop. To make matters worse, once they had squared up to each other, I could hardly go telling either side that I had only said it for a laugh and hadn't actually meant for it to end up with both of them arguing on the street! If there's a lesson to be learned here, it's this: tell the joke … but by God make sure the person you're telling it to knows it's a joke!

The Homestead

I am fully convinced that if I travelled to all corners of the earth, I wouldn't find anything that would taste even half as good as a spud that has been boiled in an old black pot over a fire made from timber and turf. There's honestly nothing like it. There was always only one way to eat them too. Anyone who has ever eaten one that way will know what I'm talking about. Once the spuds were boiled, the lot would be strained and left on a big plate in the middle of the table with the skins still intact. The skins of the spuds would almost always have burst open by the time they were boiled, especially if they were new spuds. You'd be able to see the hot steam rising from each of them, and the smell would be nothing short of divine. After you'd take the spud that looked the nicest, you'd then paste a few shavings of butter into crevice where the skin had burst. As the butter would be melting down into the hot spud, you'd sprinkle on a little salt. There was something about that combination, well you'd just devour the lot in one go if you could. I would challenge anyone to find one thing in the whole world that tastes better!

I know people can sometimes romanticise the past more than it deserves, but the truth is, the everyday staples tasted so much nicer back then. The simplest thing in the world is the cup of tea and even that tasted better back then because of the effort that used to be invested in making it. That effort is not there any more. But sure what sort of effort could there be in making a cup of tea, you might ask. Well I'll tell you the sort!

During the canvassing for the most recent election, we called into the house of a woman we knew well. While we were chatting with her, I noticed her attention to detail as she went about making the tea. She boiled the kettle, then used that water to scald the teapot in which the tea would be made. As soon as I saw her do that, I remember thinking to myself, well this woman knows what she's at because you wouldn't see many scalding a teapot these days. Next thing I saw her going to the press, and I was thinking, 'Will she or wont she?' Well, sure enough she produced a pound of tea leaves. After scooping some into the teapot, she then placed it on a low light on the gas cooker. While it was left there to draw, she went to the cupboard and picked up three fine big mugs, the real olden style. To crown it all off, she then took out the one thing you wouldn't see anywhere these days, a glass bottle of fresh creamy milk. I would have thought that you could probably count on one hand the number of people in the county who still use milk from glass bottles. It was such an unusual sight to see. As it turned out, in the area where this lady lives, there was a producer of milk who sells it in glass bottles.

I know most people won't find anything special about that whole process but that's just not the way tea is made any more. What she handed us was the kind of cup of tea that tastes amazing but that you would be hard pushed to find even in the best of restaurants these days.

Another wonderful memory I have of times gone by is of the juicy rhubarb tarts we used to enjoy. There was a time when almost every house would have a rhubarb patch in their garden, but I'd say it'd be more of a rarity these days. Home-grown rhubarb tasted second to none. It was the same with home-grown onions. I remember when people would have their onions hanging up in women's stockings to preserve them. Afterwards, you'd have these beautiful onions and my goodness they would be almost the size of small footballs. We're losing out on a lot of that nowadays. A lot of what we buy isn't organic or natural. Even though I own a shop, I would be the first person to admit that some of the ingredients in the foods we buy leave a lot to be desired.

What I love to see, and I support them wherever I can, are the honesty boxes. You would find an honesty box outside a farmhouse where there is a young person selling eggs, usually hens' eggs, but sometimes ducks' eggs as well. The young lad or lady would gather the eggs, put them out on the side of the road alongside the box. A passer-by would only need to open the lid of the box to see how much a half a dozen or a dozen would cost; they would then put the money into the box and later that day the youngster would head out and collect it. My own son Kevin used to do it when he was a child and it was always such a treat for him to see how many eggs he would have sold that day. You always know that where there's an honesty box, there's an enterprising young person behind it, and it's one of the most encouraging things I see when I'm on the road.

The Shaving of the Pig

If there is one ritual I don't exactly miss from bygone days, it's the shaving of the pig. Whenever a pig was being prepared for its departure from the world, it would always have to be shaved first. This usually took place in the farmer's house and it was almost like an event in itself in that the neighbours would come around to help with the whole operation.

Well, there was one infamous incident in which proceedings did not go as planned. When the farmer brought the pig into the house, and tied its legs together, he then placed it up on the table ready for shaving. Whatever way the ropes were tied, didn't the pig break free and start running around the house, squealing. Like a lunatic, he was. There was some amount of people in the house that night, but do you think they could catch the pig? Not a hope in hell. If they were at it yet, they still wouldn't have caught him. They decided eventually to open the back door and let the pig run out. They thought it might be easier to corner the animal if it wasn't panicking in such a confined place. The back door was opened, and out the pig ran … only to run straight around the corner and in through the front door.

I know you're wondering if the pig lived. Well, the house was turned upside down, but yes, the sprinting pig survived another day.

Turf to be Done

I love animals, and sure I suppose I'd be on OK terms with insects, but that being said, I'm on the fence about one or two of the winged ones. While I would love to see the likes of the bees being saved, I wouldn't mind a bit of mass extinction hitting the midge community. I swear to God, a turf bog would be the nicest place in the world if you could only eradicate the midges. They're horrible yokes, and when they come at you, you'd nearly rather be burning inside in the fires of hell than be under attack from the dirty things. I know most young people today would probably find this hard to believe, but if a swarm of midges descended on you while you were working in the bog, they'd nearly put you crying. You couldn't just stop working either; you'd have to suffer through them and keep going, midge bites or otherwise.

As a child, I usually went to the bog with my friends Eamon and John Sweeney. Their father, Dan, would always bring us with him. The lot of us would work hard too. Bringing home the trailer loads of turf was a big thing, almost like an occasion in itself, but the biggest highlight of the day was going into the house afterwards where Eamon and John's mother Betty would give us the feed of a lifetime. It would be a three-course meal. First, she would give each of us a big bowl of steaming hot soup along with thick slices of homemade brown bread that would be smeared with the creamiest butter. For dinner, we'd have the best of spuds, meat and vegetables. Dessert then would be something as simple as hot apple and custard. It was such a savage feed, you'd almost be paralysed after eating, you'd be so full.

Anyone who ever gave a day working in the bog will tell you that the food you eat either in the bog or after it always tastes ten times nicer than usual. Even a flask of tea, or a bottle of tea as it often was, would be the nicest you'd ever taste when it was had in the bog.

Eamon and John were gas lads growing up, and I have wonderful childhood memories of the antics that we'd get up to. We used to do a lot of cycling and sure you wouldn't know where you'd find us from one day to the next. We'd sometimes go fishing, but we would always do it late at night or very early in the morning, because the more official name for our kind of fishing was actually 'poaching'. We'd head off to the river at four or five o'clock in the morning and sure we'd always be mad nervous that we'd get caught. Thankfully we never were. We had proper fishing rods too, and I remember well the unofficial 'fishermen' who taught us how to use them properly. These lads would have been very experienced at catching fish that weren't exactly legal fair game! Despite the guidance they gave us, myself and the two Sweeneys didn't catch that many fish but on the occasion we would manage to bag ourselves a trout or a salmon, we'd be on cloud nine, thinking about how mighty we were. I'm telling you, the notions we'd have walking home! Eamon and John were also my accomplices for when we'd raid orchards as well. I mean you'd swear we were like the Kerry mafia with our carry-on. Between catching a few fish and stealing a few apples, well it was really only 'half-organised crime'.

When I think about, it amazes me how much the pace of life can change so much. Sure these days I'd hardly have time to even side-eye a fish on a plate in front of me, never mind go out and stand in a river trying to catch one. Even though I might not see them that often, the friends from my childhood still mean a lot to me. The way I look at it, you only had a certain amount of time with those people during a period that was so innocent and easy-going. No agendas, no nonsense, just genuine friendship and the daftest memories you'd laugh about time and time again.

Let Ye Stop Your Praying

Unfortunately, I can't be naming names in this particular story, but I can swear that 'tis true as God. There was a small parish in Kerry in which a large family were living, but the thing about this family is that none of them were stirring. Now, when I say they weren't 'stirring', I mean that none of the sons or daughters were showing any signs of settling down or making any shapes about getting out and getting married. There weren't even any prospects of such, would you believe. In fact, it became so evident that they weren't stirring that they started to become known around the place for it! These days, it wouldn't be unusual, but back then, it was very out of the ordinary because the done thing was to get out and get married as soon as you were legally allowed do so.

One day anyway, didn't this parish get a new priest. Back then, it was awful important for a new priest get to know his parishioners, so usually a local would bring the priest from house to house to introduce him to people. A jovial, and fairly religious, person in this particular parish had offered to bring the new priest around but what he would try to do beforehand was tip off the households they would be calling to that evening so they could be prepared and have the house cleaned up. One day he notified this family that himself and the priest would likely be calling that evening so of course once the family heard this, they made sure to keep on the lookout. That evening, they were inside in the living room when next thing, didn't they hear the rattle of the front gate. Who was it only the neighbour arriving in with the priest. Within seconds, the father issued the order that they were all to get down on their knees and start saying the Rosary so the priest would think they were awful devout and holy altogether. Sure enough, the neighbour and the priest were greeted by the

24

sight of the Rosary being said en masse. The family of course stopped praying momentarily to say hello to the priest, but the priest was so delighted at the idea of having such dedicated parishioners that he decided he would join in on their prayers.

Afterwards, he gave them all a blessing, which back then was an enormous privilege as a blessing from a new priest was a big thing to get. As he was delivering a few words following the blessing, he happened to say, 'Well, you know, they say that the family that prays together, stays together...'

Of course, the local man who had accompanied the priest to the house knew of the young ones' reputation for 'not stirring' so upon hearing the priest say those words, didn't he burst his backside laughing. The priest turned and looked at him, a bit confused by the reaction.

Right away the man quipped, 'Well, father, if that's the case, this family would want to stop praying together so!'

Would You Like to Dance?

When I was growing up, our local dance hall, the Gala Ballroom, was owned by our school headmaster, Master Hickey. It was a unique place in that it was one of the few dance halls in all of Ireland that had a properly sprung floor. In other words, it had a spring-like mechanism underneath it so when everyone was dancing, there'd be some give in the boards. Of course no alcohol was served, only minerals, tea, and things like Snack bars. Some mighty dances were held there, but the people that attended them were equally memorable.

I remember Dermot Coffey was always in charge of collecting the money at the door. He was so honest and so trustworthy, you could give him the Crown Jewels, and sure he'd give them back to you in better condition than he got them. Dermot was also an extremely industrious man; one of those people that was always way ahead of their time. When nobody else had a guesthouse, Dermot and his wife Ella had a guesthouse. He held down a full-time profession too. If he hadn't enough on his plate with that, he also had the unusual job of being both a pig buyer and a pig grader. You'd often hear the story of the one little piggy that went to the market, and the one little piggy that stayed at home – well, Dermot's job was to decide which path each little piggy went down. Each morning before starting work, Dermot would head up to the piggery and grade the ones that were ready for sale, and the ones that would have to wait a bit longer. He was an expert at it. When he wasn't dealing with the pigs, he would always be wearing a suit with a colourful shirt and tie at a time when hardly any man dressed like that.

Tadgh Quill, the great character I wrote about earlier in the story 'Fire in the Trenches', was another frequent dance hall patron. A mighty waltzer, he always used to take to the floor with a can in his hand (but not that kind of can, there was no alcohol, remember). The can he'd be holding would be a can of a powdery substance, which was actually Luxe Soap Flakes. He would shake it all around the floor, so people could slide around more as they were waltzing. Dancers loved it because it helped them move with ease. Master Hickey, the owner of the dance hall, used to play in a band with my father and on many an occasion they would take to the stage in the Gala Ballroom. They actually played at many a dance hall around Kerry, not just Master Hickey's. You see, they loved going to dances but they didn't always have the price of the petrol to take them there. By being in a band, however, the money they would earn from a booking would cover the cost of the petrol. They also didn't have to worry about the price of the entrance fee because they would be the ones providing the entertainment and so would get in for free.

I remember I was around seven or eight years of age when I was first allowed go to a dance. It was during the time of some fleadh ceol or carnival. I'll never forget one night in particular. I think I was about twelve at the time. The boys had all congregated to one side of the hall, the girls were on the other. Typical old-fashioned dance hall protocol. As I was looking across to where there was a gathering of girls, one young one, Catherine Lynch, stood out from the crowd. Well, to say I couldn't take my eyes off her would be a big understatement. Common sense would suggest that I would just head over and ask her to dance but social rules tended to trump all sorts of sense, and at that time, the one thing you wouldn't dare attempt to do was cross the floor and ask a girl to dance. First of all, you'd be terrified that the older people there would think you were missing a bit in the head department. Second, you would be afraid your friends would see you because the ribbing you'd get over it would be something out of this world.

This girl was gorgeous, though, so I stood there for ages weighing up the situation in my head. After a desperate amount of humming and hawing, I decided to cross the floor. I didn't go telling the lads that were with me either. There were some great characters there like the aforementioned Thomas Gill, Donal Callaghan, Denis O'Sullivan, Kevin Reilly, people who I would still to this day be great friends with. Friendship aside, I knew they would give me an awful ribbing if I crossed the floor and asked this girl to dance. Anyway, I threw caution to the wind and started to make my way over.

As I was walking, something occurred to me. What if she said no? If that happened, I'd be absolutely destroyed, mortified! In the few steps it took to reach her side of the hall, my twelve-year-old brain had me convinced it would be going down in history as the biggest natural disaster in all of Kerry. I'd be the fella that crossed the floor, put himself up for public ridicule, and was shot down! Refused! Rejected! I'd honestly say I was shaking with the fear. I went across and faced her. 'Will you dance?' I asked her. After what seemed like an eternity of her looking at me like I was mad, she said she would. I was shocked, but so too were my friends, and probably the rest of the dance hall as well. Once she said yes, I realised that was only one problem out of the way. The next problem facing me was that I had just asked this girl out for a waltz … but I didn't know how to waltz. In hindsight, I was setting myself up for a right fall altogether.

Over the space of I'd say twenty seconds, I worried about everything from whether my nerves would be contained enough to actually be able to dance with her, what I would say to her while we were dancing, and what everyone else's reaction would be. I was so nervous about all the eyes that were on us, you'd honestly swear we were after getting married and heading out for our first dance. The minute we started dancing, though, she was lovely and chatty; very easy to get on with. We started talking right away and everything went fine. Sure once we started talking about school, innocent sort of stuff, we nearly didn't stop for the rest of the night.

That night is like a photograph in my head to this day. She was around the same age as myself, and we ended up meeting again on a number of occasions for other dances. I mean it in the most innocent way, but it was almost like the highlight of the dance when I'd go in and see her there. It was a real childhood romance. Would you believe, not only are we still very good friends to this day, she married another very good friend of mine, Simon O'Connor. Simon is a highly respectable, hardworking man, and today himself and Catherine are known throughout the county for their prize-winning cattle. A nicer couple you couldn't meet.

The Clergy, the Dance Hall and the Circuit Court

You know, isn't it honestly mad the way things used to be? In 1948, the Lake House dance hall was started in Tuosist, and the local clergy were so determined to stop it opening that they brought the matter all the way to the Circuit Court. I'm not sure what kind of debauchery they were afraid of taking place there, but they tried their damnedest to put a halt to the hall and the dances that were planned for it. Fortunately the Circuit Court gave the local clergy no soot whatsoever and all attempts to rid the village of the dance hall were unsuccessful.

The same dance hall, would you believe, sadly closed its doors for the final time in the summer of 2019. For its final night, the owners held a ceilí dance, so I popped in for one last time. While I was there that night, what struck me was the amazing way in which things come full circle. When my father was a young man, he and his band regularly played on the stage of that dance hall. That night, I met three different couples who in the 1960s had met in the dance hall and most likely danced on occasion to the music of my father and his band.

While the Lake House dance hall may now be closed, I'm fully convinced it's only for the foreseeable future. As I said, things always come full circle, and in the years to come, who knows, but those dance hall doors may well be thrown open to the crowds once again.

Rambling House

I hope we never see an end to the rambling houses of Ireland. I love going to rambling houses. Usually a rambling house takes place in a community centre. An absolute load of locals would be there, and each one would take a turn to do their party piece. Then during the break, everyone would enjoy tea and maybe a few slices of barm brack.

In recent times, I visited a number of rambling houses along with my son, Jackie. The last night I was in one, I counted around 140 people in attendance, and I remember thinking that if I'd had a choice between being at the fanciest show in the country and being at a rambling house in Kerry, I'd choose the rambling house any day. The banisteoir or whoever was in charge would call out the name of the person up next to do their party piece, and honest to God, some of the performances would be frighteningly good. You'd almost be excited to see the next performance before the one in front of you had even finished!

Another tradition I enjoy, and I think this one might be exclusive to Kerry, would be the Biddies. Kerry is probably the only place in the country where the mention of the word Biddy doesn't stir up memories of Glenroe. The Biddies are a group that go around to various places, pubs and the likes, wearing straw hats and white costumes. It takes place over the course of ten days or so. Whenever they would go into a place, they would dance and play the accordion, all while collecting for charities. Over the years they have collected thousands for different causes.

I remember going to Biddy nights long ago where there'd be dances inside in people's houses. Those were some great nights. It wasn't about drinking either, in fact it was the opposite, as a lot of the Biddies are from the pioneer association in Beaufort. We need to try and reinvigorate that type of social interaction and entertainment. I'll be damned if I let the iPhones kill that element of Irish society.

Years ago, the home was where relatives, friends and neighbours would call in of a night and the entertainment would be singing, dancing and storytelling. And do you know something? It was more enjoyable than any fancy home entertainment system you'd get today. Times have moved on, but when it comes to certain things, I think the times need to be reversed. The reputation of the Irish for being sociable came from all the craic we'd create for ourselves when we didn't have so much as a radio or a television to be creating it for us. These days, a lot of us don't even know our neighbours, and that's something I find incredibly sad and disheartening.

Another thing that has changed a great deal is the family. Families have become smaller, which is fine in one way, because in fairness, if people don't want to have children, then that's their choice, but there's great power and strength in the family unit. Speaking from a place of nostalgia, I find it sad that we have said goodbye to the days when you would see families with twelve, fourteen, even sixteen children. I believe that children who come from big families, well there's a special type of ambitious drive that's almost in their DNA. Look at Bill Cullen, who came from a large family, and the success he enjoyed as a businessman?

I remember many years back a lovely Kerry couple, Nora and the late Johnny Kelly, had nineteen children. Sadly, at the time of writing this book, their eldest son Eamon passed away. The one thing that never ceases to amaze me about the Kelly family is the future potential that now exists there. The union of two people created nineteen children, but think about the children that all nineteen might then go on to have, and so on and so forth. My goodness, in a number of generations, they'd have enough people brought into this world to form a type of army ... they could have become a county on their own.

Sure at the very least they'd have a football team.

A Sporty Escort

I know full well where your mind went when you first read the title of this story. Into the gutter is where it went. Well, take it back out of there, because the only kind of escort I'd be talking about, or have any interest in, is the kind with wheels.

Ever since I was knee high, I've had a love of cars. I remember there was a great man in our parish who gave his life on the oil rigs. Whenever he was home, the one thing he always had was a very good car. I remember when he had an RS 2000. Now, 'twasn't everyone that had one of these. You'd hardly have a Ford Escort, never mind an RS 2000 Escort, but this man had one, and for as long as I live, I'll never forget the first night he arrived into the village in it. That was my first time being up close to an RS 2000. Sure every young fella within a ten-mile radius descended upon Kilgarvan. There were no mobile phones that time, but still the word got out that this flashy car was in Kilgarvan. It was parked on the side of the street, and at one stage, there must have been thirty or forty young lads standing around it trying to rub it and get a look at it. To even see one of these cars in person was an experience in itself, so of course anyone who got near it automatically wanted to touch it. By the time the owner came out, his poor car was covered in paw marks.

To this day, I've maintained a love for old vintage cars, but I especially love the old Anglia motors. My Uncle Dan always had one of them and they were, and still are, just beautiful. Another man who has a car I love – a beautiful vintage-style Volkswagen Beetle – is Mick O'Neil. Mick and his wife Anne own the Railway Tavern pub just outside Tralee and are lifelong friends of mine. The distinctive feature about Mick is that he has a long beard right down to his belly button. The vintage-style Volkswagen he drives is actually his everyday car. With his long beard and glasses, he's a novel sight to see on the road when he's behind the wheel of such a beautiful car, so much so that one day as he was driving along, wasn't he spotted on the road by someone who happened to be working in the marketing department of AIB. They thought he looked mighty and could see the potential of his image, so they used him and his Volkswagen in an ad campaign. I'd say the ad must have run for about a year or two. His face was on buses, in newspapers, everywhere you saw an AIB ad, it was likely Mick's face and beard staring back at you!

Mick is awful good craic and if you ever call into his bar, you can tell him I sent you. I remember one time outside his bar, he organised the re-enactment of the old Irish tradition of balancing upside down on top of a heap of turf that was piled up high on a horse cart. The purpose of this tradition was to show how steady and even the load of turf was, and it was one that Mick's own ancestors would have carried out time and time again. In honour of the memory, he asked a local young man to help recreate the scene. My father and myself were actually both there for this entertaining re-enactment. We thought it was gas craic altogether, but what I would really love to know is what the passing tourists made of the sight of a long-bearded Irish man giving instructions to a young man trying to balance himself upside down on a rail of turf on the back of a horse and cart!

From the Dáil to the Maternity Ward

If I'm ever having a chat with a Kilgarvan local, and I mention my own young lad, Kevin, I usually always have to refer to him as 'Small Kevin' so as to differentiate him from another local Kevin. The other Kevin, 'Big Kevin', is a man by the name of Kevin O'Reilly, another lad I went to school with. He now owns the aforementioned Reilly's bar. Kevin is an accountant by trade but also a very hardworking farmer, and his farmyard would be behind my house.

I remember one evening when I was on the road down from Dublin, big Kevin phoned and explained one of his cows was in trouble. She was calving and needed a caesarean section. I put down the foot to the floor and as soon as I landed at my house, I threw off the suit and fired on my old clothes as fast as I could. Out I went to Kevin's sheds where a mighty vet, Donal Murphy, was there along with a couple of other neighbours. Sure no sooner had I arrived than I fell in helping Donal with the usual things like boiling the water, making sure the bedding was clean, helping in any way I could. Whatever way I was on my knees, holding a needle and thread after having scalded it so it was clean for the closing-up, Donal took one look at me and said, 'God, lads, isn't this great? Local and national democracy at work! One minute he's on his way home from the Dáil in a suit, the next he's on his knees helping with a caesarean section!'

One former classmate who certainly isn't on his knees stitching up postpartum cows is a man by the name of Noelie O'Sullivan. It's funny how some things pan out in life. When I was in school, everyone had a nickname but it's rare that someone would go on to live up to their nickname as an adult. Well, Noelie hailed from the O'Sullivan Cooper family in Ardtully, an extremely bright family; very intelligent lot altogether. Like his family, Noelie was fierce brainy, so one day didn't I nickname him 'the professor'. Low and behold, what do you think his actual title is today? Sure isn't he a professor over in Oxford University!

Another lad that stands out when I look back on my schooling days is Donal Callaghan. Sometimes when you have a think about those formative years, you remember some people for all the wrong reasons, while others you remember for all the right ones. Well, Donal was one of the latter. You know the kind of lad that always has a 'happy head' on him? That was Donal. No matter what the hour of the day or night it was, he always had a smile on his face. It almost became his speciality. We could be on the bus perished with the cold on a morning when the road would almost be cracking with the frost, and Donal would be sitting there happy out, as if he were on a beach in Greece. We could be drenched to the skin after having togged out underneath a bush, and about to head to a football game in the pouring rain, and Donal would be walking along with a grand smile on his face. He was the sort that would always put you in good form because he was always the one with an outlook on the bright side, regardless of the situation. I firmly believe people like that deserve to be extremely lucky and successful in life. Sadly for us all in Ireland, Donal saw his future in America. Today, he is a very successful builder and contractor, and no doubt he's brightening up his corner of America in the same way he brightened up Kilgarvan.

Your Usual, Bertha?

There isn't a rural pub in the country whose bar counter hasn't seen its fair share of strange and unusual characters, but I'd go so far as to say that there's only one pub where there's been a cow standing at the counter alongside the locals, sipping on her own pint of Guinness. If I'm not mistaken, she was also partial to a drop of whiskey and poitín as well on occasion. The cow, whose name was Big Bertha and whose owner was a fine Sneem man called Jerome O'Leary, had become a bit of a celebrity after she started breaking records left, right and centre. She was featured in the *Guinness Book of Records* for having been the oldest Droimeann cow ever, and after having produced thirty-nine calves during her lifetime, she was credited with the breeding record also.

Before Bertha was officially entered into the book of records, however, she had become known for being Ireland's oldest cow, so in 1992, on her 48th birthday in fact, Gay Byrne's radio show sent Joe Duffy down to Bertha's local, the Blackwater Tavern in Kerry, to meet the birthday girl herself. A big celebration was thrown in Bertha's honour and naturally, she was brought into the pub where she was stood a complimentary pint. 'Twas only right, to be fair. Even *Hello!* magazine gave her birthday a mention.

One year, Bertha was chosen to be the grand marshal for Sneem's St Patrick's Day parade. Before she hit the road to lead the parade, however, her owner Jerome sensed she was a bit nervous. He knew just what to do. He would always give her a little taste of whiskey or poitín just to fortify her nerves in case she started to become alarmed by the crowds of people, all of whom would be vying to meet her. On this occasion, a drop of whiskey did the trick, and sure after a minute or two she was back to her old self. In fairness, it was her birthday so now you could hardly go begrudging the poor girl a little tipple early in the afternoon.

As you can imagine, newspapers both in Ireland and abroad started to pick up on Bertha's unusual story, which of course generated even more recognition. Now, Jerome was a smart man, and he could see there was a fascination with Bertha, so he decided to put her fame to mighty use and started organising her personal appearances at fairs and shows and the likes, all in a bid to raise money for cancer research. Over her lifetime, herself and Jerome raised thousands upon thousands for a great cause. I could be wrong, but I think the overall total wasn't far off £100,000, which was incredible. At one point, there was talk of possibly bringing Bertha on a charity fundraising trip to New York.

Sadly, on the morning of New Year's Eve 1993, just three months shy of her 49th birthday, Bertha, God be good to her, left us for her eternal reward and is now grazing the green pastures in the sky. Looking back, we honestly should have held a day of mourning for her. That girl was like a local institution. As was only right, Bertha was waked in her beloved local, the Blackwater Tavern, on the night of New Year's Eve. There wasn't room to move with the number of people who turned out to pay their respects. In fact, Turtle Bunbury, a well-known travel writer who happened to stumble upon the momentous occasion by sheer chance after he and three friends stopped off for a quick drink, later wrote of the wake and how the pub had been 'packed to suffocation' for it.

Bertha's story doesn't end there either. Following her passing, Jerome decided that Bertha should not be buried, but rather immortalised for eternity, so he brought her to a taxidermist and had her preserved. After Jerome himself sadly passed, Bertha was given to Jerome's friend and neighbour George Kelly, and to this day, she resides at his Hazel Fort farm in Beaufort where she is on view as the world's most famous cow.

Rebel Sheep Dippers

Over the years, the government has banned many things, but it was always for the common good. Things like plastic bags, smoking in bars, that sort of craic. The one ban, however, that I wasn't too happy about was that of black sheep dip. My father, God rest him, was even more unimpressed than I was with the ban. The dip had been done away with on environmental grounds. It was strong, which meant for sheep farmers it was mighty stuff altogether. A lesser strength of dip was brought out, but sure of course it wasn't half as good as the stuff that had been banned.

I'll never forget one evening, as we were driving out to Dingle for a meeting, I noticed my father in the passenger seat scrunching up his face and sniffing as though he was getting a whiff of something. I still to this day don't know how he could smell anything as all the car windows were rolled up at the time, and we weren't exactly driving at a snail's pace either.

'Do you smell it?' he asked.

'Smell what?' I said.

'Stop! Stop the car!'

I pulled to a stop.

'Turn the car around,' he said. 'Pull in there.'

Out he jumps from the car and straight away starts looking over across the road. Sure enough, there was a farmer there dipping sheep. The thing about black dip is that the smell of it was unique; it had a very distinctive odour, and as we were driving along, despite the windows being shut, hadn't my father got the smell of it. Over he went to the man using it.

'In the honour of God man, where did you get that black sheep dip?'

The poor man nearly went pale. He was sure he was in awful trouble for using a banned substance. 'I had a good bit left over, Jackie,' he said. 'I just thought I'd use it up; I find it better than the new stuff.'

Next thing my father leaned in, and, lowering his voice, quietly asked, 'Any chance you'd give me a bit of it? I'm lost without it since the ban.'

The very nice man ended up giving my father a few gallons of it and off we headed for the meeting in Dingle, himself as happy as Larry. I wish this is where the story ended, but no. To my misfortune, the black dip left its mark that evening. In my car, to be precise. As we were driving to Dingle, didn't a bit of the dip spill inside in the boot of the car. It soaked into the carpet and for two years after that, my car was filled with the strongest smell of black sheep dip. If you stuck your head in the car, you'd swear I was after being dosed in it myself. I must have diluted it with water a thousand times and the damn thing was still every bit as strong – if anything, it was getting worse.

My father and I used travel everywhere together. I could probably write a book alone on the things that happened while we were on the road. I remember a few years back, we both had identical cars, and I mean 100% identical. There'd be some nights when we'd be arriving home from meetings; it could be two in the morning and we wouldn't know which one of us was to get out or stay inside because we'd have no idea whose car we were in. I would always be driving, though. Himself would be the passenger seat driver, although there was one occasion where he found himself on traffic duty.

Myself and my father were driving through the Conor Pass one day with our good friend Arthur Lenihan. We were going from the Dingle Show to an event in Tralee, and as we made our way down the other side of the Conor Pass, didn't we notice a pile of cars coming up against us. Now, if you've ever been in the Conor Pass, you'll know that in certain parts, two cars can't pass. Straight away, my father hops out of the car and starts directing traffic. We'd be ready to make a burst and get on a couple of feet, when next thing another car would appear. We'd get by one car with the height of scraping, but the roaring and screeching that was coming from my father was something else. You'd see another car coming around the corner and all you'd see next was my father putting his hands up to his head, 'Oh sweet Jesus, God in heaven above, another one of them!' I'd almost swear there was an echo of his voice booming out through the valley. Of course, we were inside in the car dying laughing at all this racket and sure the more we laughed, the more annoyed and cross himself would become.

But getting back to when we had the identical cars. So one day anyway, my father and I were driving from Cork when we met a desperate flood on the road at Ballyvourney. All the cars were turning back, so, being in the driving seat, I asked himself what he thought we should do. He was looking at his watch anxiously because the meeting we were heading to was an important one and he wanted to be on time for it.

'Do you know what?' he said, 'Chance it!'

Slowly I started to drive through it. The water was up so high, the Mercedes star logo on the bonnet was making a design in the ripples of the water as we were making our way through it. If you opened the door, the flood of water would've come in on top of you, and if we even so much as stalled at all, we'd have been goosed! Somehow, we managed to make our way through the flood and as we were driving out the other side, I happened to say to my father, 'I hope the auld car will be alright after going through all that water … but sure won't you know for yourself later on?'

'Ha?' he said back to me, a look of pure confusion on his face. 'How do you mean I'll know later on?'

'When you're driving it yourself. Sure this is your car!'

'This is my car?' came the fright of a roar back, almost as loud as when he was directing traffic in the Conor Pass. 'Jesus, God man, if I had known it was my car, I wouldn't have had you chance it! I wouldn't have had you chance it at all!'

Here he was after putting the car in severe danger but only because he thought it was my car when all along it was his own!

The Late Jimmy Breen and His Hooting Hearse

A lorry load of cattle is a difficult feat to manage at the best of times, but a lorry load of shtone mad cattle is another battle altogether. This my father found out for himself one horrible wet night in Sneem when he was on his way home to Kilgarvan. He had bought some cattle at a fair in Cahersiveen that day and was transporting them home in a bad auld lorry on a bad auld road when he sensed something was wrong. When he got out of the lorry, didn't he realise the legs of the cattle were after going down through the floor of the body of the lorry. In other words, the timber floor had been rotting, and gave way under the weight of the herd. There were legs out all sides. You wouldn't know if you were in a lorry or a brothel. It was an awful predicament to find yourself in, especially when you're on your own on the side of the road, never mind it being a bad wet night and a load of animals going mental behind you.

All my father could do was go to the nearest house and ask for assistance. Whose house was it, only that of James Breen. Now James has since left this world, God be good to him, but what happened on this particular night was not only a reflection of how genuine a man he was, it was also how he and my father became firm lifelong friends.

My father knocked on the door, waking up poor James as it was now all hours of the morning. Now, many a man would eff you out of it for disturbing their night's sleep, but not James. He answered the door and greeted my father as if it were the middle of the day.

'I'm in an awful way,' my father explained to him. 'I have a lorry load of cattle and aren't they after going down through the floor of the lorry. I don't know what in the name of God I'm going to do with them.'

'Well Jackie, I have a meadow there, but it has been closed off for hay …'

What you need to know here is that this meadow was the only good field James had, and without it, he'd have no hay for the winter. What do you think he said to my father, though?

'Jackie, there's only one thing we can do. We'll have to put the cattle in the meadow; it's the only piece of ground I have that's fenced properly.'

My father was taken aback. 'Sure we can't put them in there, James! They'll destroy the meadow; you'll have no hay for the winter.'

'Lookit, we've no choice,' said James. 'If we let them off up into the hill, you'll never put them in again!'

That man sacrificed his field for my father's cattle. You don't forget something like that, and let me tell you, my father never did. From that day forward, the two were good friends.

As luck would have it, I was then fortunate enough to become good friends with James's son, Jimmy. Jimmy would have been predominantly a Fianna Fáil man over the years but in 1997 he was one of the first lieutenants to say he was leaving Fianna Fáil and going off with Jackie Healy-Rae. Roll on 1999, when I first ran for the council, and Jimmy took time off work without hesitation and hit the road canvassing with me. He gave week after week, month after month, canvassing thousands upon thousands of people, and ultimately helped get me elected.

Jimmy fitted so many different lives into his own life. As well as being a building contractor and a farmer, he drove an artic lorry on the continent for the great Joe C Keating of Cahersiveen, a great employer in Kerry. Jimmy also spent time in the hospitality sector, working in hotels mainly. He worked with Catherine and the late Tom O'Carroll in the then Ringside Rest Hotel in Cahersiveen, and also in the Park Hotel in Kenmare, which is owned by the famous Brennan brothers. His job was being in charge of the maintenance. I remember one night when someone said to Jimmy, 'Aren't you very lucky you got a job in the Park Hotel?' and ever the humble character, Jimmy's answer was, 'My goodness do you know I never thought you'd be so foolish as to come out with a statement like that! Wouldn't you phrase it properly and say how lucky they were in the Park Hotel to have me working for them!' His modesty never hindered him. I held Jimmy in the highest respect and cherished every hour I worked with him. Very sadly, he passed away as I was writing this book.

A week before Jimmy went into hospital, I had the privilege of spending the day canvassing with him. He wasn't feeling 100%, but right or wrong, he wanted to be out and about meeting the voters with me. What I used do was drive up outside a house with him, but I wouldn't let him get out of the car. Instead I would keep the heater on low so his toes would be kept warm, and he'd roll down the window at every house and salute the people we were canvassing. Everyone we canvassed would always be delighted to see him.

Not long after that, Jimmy passed away in Cork University Hospital. For the final journey back to Sneem, the undertaker Brendan O'Leary of Castlecove, who was a great man for attention to detail, was given a number of requests by the family, one of them being that when he was passing through Kilgarvan with Jimmy in the hearse, he had to do the exact same thing that Jimmy would always do whenever he was passing by the Healy-Rae shop. He had to hoot the horn and wave out the window.

Sure enough, as the hearse passed the shop, Brendan the undertaker started hooting the horn and waving out the window. At the time, there were a good few people going in and out of the shop, as well as people getting petrol. Of course, locals who knew the story would have said to themselves, 'Well that's Jimmy Breen giving the final salute before he goes home to be buried,' but to the many people who might not have known, tourists and the likes, they'd have been completely confused as to why this undertaker was hooting the horn, smiling and waving out the window at no one in particular, and all with the coffin in the back of the hearse and a procession of cars behind him. Well that was Jimmy Breen going out in style.

Jimmy was waked at his home for three nights with his wife Mary and their family, and I was very glad to have been there each night. His funeral was like a major celebration of his life. Thousands of people came from all over to pay their respects; the volume of people was a testament to his popularity.

At the time, there was a council election taking place and we had three Healy-Raes running in it: my son Jackie, my nephew Johnny and my niece Maura. While Jimmy was being waked, his wife, Mary, being the great woman that she is, slipped three Healy-Rae canvass cards into the inside pocket of his coat. 'He'll do a bit of canvassing on the other side for them,' she smiled. Even in death, Jimmy Breen was the most loyal supporter you could get.

The Nuns' Nudist Beach

If you're not familiar with Ballybunion, the one thing you need to know before reading this story is that there are three beaches there: the Nuns' Beach, the Women's Beach and the Men's Beach. Well, one day, didn't my father decide that one of the three beaches, the Nuns' Beach, should be turned into a nudist beach. It was the most private of the three and he figured if any of them were suitable for a nudist colony, it would be that one. He even went as far as putting a motion down for the proposal in the council chamber.

His friend, the former senator Dan Kiely, was a councillor in Ballybunion at the time, and completely against the idea because he felt it was a family beach. In response, he put down a counter motion objecting to it. Given that such a beach could be good publicity for Ballybunion, Dan of course was encouraged to reconsider his objection.

'Have you something against it?' one of the council members asked him.

'I haven't,' replied Dan, 'sure wasn't I at a nudist beach in Baden-Baden there recently? Ballybunion isn't the place for one because it's a seaside resort for families.'

The motion went down anyway and Dan followed with his counter motion.

During the council meeting, my father let fly. He brought up Dan's visit to Baden-Baden, but sure in the midst of all the shouting, didn't he forget himself and instead of saying Baden-Baden, he said Beijing.

'Kiely!' he said, 'what have you against the nudist beach? Sure weren't you at one in Beijing and here you are coming in complaining about the idea of having one in Ballybunion?'

The motion made headlines in *The Kerryman* newspaper, and in the article, my father's 'Beijing' remarks to Dan were quoted. As could be expected, the unusual story caught the attention of the national media, and one of the broadcasters who phoned my father and Dan looking for an interview was Marian Finucane. When they went live, Dan was on one end of the phone and Jackie was on the other. I'm recalling from memory here, but it went something like this:

Jackie: 'There's Kiely now, objecting to a nudist beach and he out at one himself in Beijing.'

Marion: 'No Jackie, I think it was Baden-Baden.'

Jackie: 'Marian, aren't I telling you it was Beijing! I'm reading it out of *The Kerryman*. It was over in Beijing he was.'

Sure it was the mistake in his own quote that he was reading in the newspaper!

When you think about it, the motion was a very forward-thinking one. At that time, people were shy about exposing any part of themselves, so for a Kerry politician to come out and suggest that we transform a beach into one specifically for nudists, well it's not something you'd be expecting at your standard council meeting.

To be honest, my father was always ahead of his time when it came to the unusual ideas he would devise. I remember when he had the idea of edible chip trays for chippers. That way, when customers were finished eating their chips, they wouldn't just throw the plastic tray on the ground, the tray would be a functional one as it too could be eaten. This was about thirty years ago, and when I think about it, and how 'plastic conscious' everyone has become, I realise just how ahead of his time he was.

Unfortunately he didn't get around to pursuing the idea, so in the end, the chip boxes remained inedible. The Nuns' Beach also stayed as it was. If nudists wanted to strip, they simply had to find another spot or else swap Ballybunion for Baden-Baden.

Nothing Like A Bit of Blaggarding

Aloysius 'Weeshie' Fogarty was the ultimate interviewer. A great character, and a very intelligent, witty one at that, he'd always get the most out of you. I always maintained that if I had a question and could only get the answer from Google or Weeshie Fogarty, I'd honestly be miles better off asking Weeshie.

If you had an interest in GAA, Weeshie's name is one you will likely recognise, both as a former player and as a sports reporter. Even though he started out his working life as a psychiatric nurse, he went on to develop a great name for himself as a sports commentator. His Radio Kerry show *Terrace Talk*, on which he would interview various personalities, was hugely popular. I remember Weeshie had been on to me for ages about the prospect of interviewing myself, my father, who was a TD at the time, and my brother Danny, who was a councillor. You'd imagine it would be easy enough to get the three of us in for an interview, but it was downright next to impossible. When it would suit one, it wouldn't suit another.

We were going around in circles until one night, by some miracle, we were all free to do the interview with Weeshie, so we met up in Tralee and headed into the studio for the show. It was a very nice, light-hearted affair and everything was going perfect in the interview until Weeshie looked at my father and said with a jovial smile on his face, 'Jackie, I believe you have a new title now?'

'And what title is that, Weeshie?' my father asked, no clue as to what Weeshie was about to say.

Next thing Weeshie, with a very innocent look on his face, replied, 'Sure Jackie, you're the oldest man in the Dáil now!'

I looked at Weeshie. Then I looked at my brother. And then I glanced over at my father and all I could do was look up at the ceiling and pray for the best, because all I was thinking was, 'Oh sugar, what in the name of God is going to be said next?'

Well, my father started twisting in his seat, always a sure-fire sign that he was getting ready for an attack. He moved his head from side to side, started twisting this way and that way, and next thing you know, there was no more smiling.

'Well now, Weeshie,' he began, 'I don't know about that. That wouldn't be exactly factual now, I'd say.'

The thing is, anything that came out of Weeshie's mouth would undoubtedly be 100% factual.

'I don't think you'd be right about that, Weeshie,' he continued. 'For instance ...'

Well he went on to reel off a list of names of the people in the Dáil who were reportedly older than he was, but the one problem with every person he named was that they were definitely, without a shadow of a doubt, a good five, if not ten, years younger than himself. He was adamant, of course, that they were all older and that in no way was he the oldest man in the Dáil. Weeshie got the hint that his question had touched a nerve, and I can tell you he wasn't long deflecting the ball away from the issue.

Fast forward to when we were heading back out to the car in the underground carpark. All that was going through my head was the piece where Weeshie mentioned the age. I knew it would be driving my father mental, and I knew the best thing to do would be to distract him with a different subject and instead say nothing at all about Weeshie, but to be honest, a little bit of devilment in me decided to test the waters.

So I turned to him, and with a smile on my face, I said, 'Do you know something? Wasn't that very nice, that whole interview? Isn't Weeshie a great man altogether?' Well, my father turned and looked at me. If there was a colour scale for levels of temper, the shade his face was going would have been at the 'burning red' end.

'Weeshie? Weeshie?' he started, huffing and puffing, his voice getting louder with each 'Weeshie'. 'Well, I'll tell you about Weeshie now! He's a damn fine feckin' blaggard if you ask me.'

Truth be told, my father had the best of time and the height of respect for Weeshie. Sure he wouldn't have done the interview only for he really liked him. Unfortunately, I never got to recall that story for Weeshie himself as he passed away in 2018, but I did tell his family about it and they got mileage out of the image of my father going mental over Weeshie's observation about his age.

P**s Talk on the Canvass Trail

I'm not one for vulgarity, and maybe that title should have been a bit stronger, but that title is the only one suitable for this story. When you read it, you'll see why. My father and I have always been great friends with the Callaghan family who own Killarney's Fáilte Hotel. The late Dermot Callaghan was a great man altogether and would have been a close ally of my father. The two of them used to have fierce-but-friendly battles over politics. You had to stand your ground and give as good as you got with my father, and by God, Dermot did that. He was always very factual and very blunt. He would tell it as it was, and he would usually be smoking one of those really thick cigars while he was doing so.

I remember one day myself and Dermot were out canvassing for my father; we were on the Upper Lewis Road in Killarney, where there was a bit of a walk between the houses but not enough that you'd need a car. We were walking for ages, and at the time, I had a leg brace that ran from my foot the whole way up my leg, stopping right up underneath my 'downstairs department' so to speak. Now, if you read the first book, *Time to Talk*, you'll know I gave four years on crutches and a further couple of years wearing that mercifully awkward leg brace, but if you want to know why I spent all those years smathering with crutches and leg braces, well I'm afraid there's nothing for it other than to go and read the first book!

Anyway, as we were walking along, I felt something wasn't quite right with my leg brace. It was getting awful uncomfortable but then something started to feel a bit 'off'. I couldn't tell what it was, I just knew something had gone very, very, wrong down there. To make matters worse, it was also a really hot day. Eventually it reached a point where there was no ignoring it any further, so I turned to Dermot.

'We'll have to go back to the Fáilte, Dermot, there's something gone fierce wrong down below.'

'How'd you mean something's gone wrong?' he asked.

'To be honest, I don't know,' I explained. 'My leg sort of feels very wet. There's something gone wrong with me, but I don't know what in the name of God it is!'

Between the clammy weather, all the walking, and the anxiety of what was going on inside my leg brace, I wasn't feeling too good, and starting to get a bit hot and bothered, so we put a temporary pause on the canvassing and headed back to the Fáilte. In we went, and sure of course as soon as we were there, I made my way to the bathroom to see if I could sort things out. There I was trying to be as discreet as I could while making my way up the stairs to the toilets, when next thing I hear some fella asking Dermot why we were back so soon from canvassing. With absolutely no regard for volume or privacy, Dermot replies, 'I dunno! That fecker Michael has gone upstairs. You know, I think he's after pissing himself on the side of the road! Wouldn't you think he'd pick a bush or something?'

What had actually gone wrong is that the stocking inside my leg brace had fallen down slightly, causing the brace to rub against the skin while we were walking. The friction led to the skin tearing and bleeding a good bit. I think it must have nicked a vessel or something because the blood was everywhere. Anyway, there was canvassing to be done, so I quickly bandaged the area and tried to make myself comfortable enough to get back on the road again.

You'd often hear of fellas putting their blood, sweat and tears into the election campaign. Well I certainly put the blood in, and the tears weren't long following when I heard Dermot telling the bar I had wet myself. Down I went into the bar and sure no sooner had I walked in when all eyes went straight to the private department to see if there was any evidence of what Dermot had been saying. If I'm not mistaken, there were also a few mutterings along the lines of, 'Is he in the habit of pissing himself or what?'

I'd say anyone who canvassed with Dermot had an anecdote or a story to tell about their time with him. I remember when Dermot went out canvassing in Dingle with Arthur Linehan. That night, they joined my father and I for a meeting to catch up.

'Dermot, how did you get on today?' my father asked

'Very good, Jackie, very good altogether. Before we left, we went into the bar, and Jackie, I stood them all inside there a drink.'

Next thing Arthur Lenihan piped up. 'You did, but sure there was only one man inside in the bar!'

'That's right!' said Dermot back, 'And sure didn't I buy him a pint? So I'm right, I did stand a drink to everyone in the bar! I stood everyone that was in there.'

An Expensive Pint

Every rural area has a rare sort of character that can get away with a level of devilment that most others would nearly be shot for. Dermot Callaghan was definitely one of those people. I'd say the most famous story about him is the one that was told at his graveside. In the Fáilte one day, an American woman who was a little worse for wear was coming down the stairs when she missed the last couple of steps and fell in a heap. Dermot saw the whole thing and immediately rushed over to make sure she was OK. She was fine, remarkably, no injuries whatsoever, but Dermot was worried his hotel would be liable for damages so what did he do only link arms with the woman and escort her across the road to Scott's Hotel, which was owned by his good friend, Maurice O'Donoghue. Dermot put her sitting on the bottom step of the stairs in Scott's and went into the bar where he ordered a stiff brandy – not that the woman needed it, mind you, because God love her, she was already facing the mother of all hangovers the next morning. Teresa, the barmaid, was serving.

'Dermot, when did you start drinking brandy?' she asked. 'Sure, you only drink Scotch!'

'Oh, it's not for me, Teresa!' Dermot replied, nonchalant as could be. 'No, this is for the woman that fell down your stairs there. I think ye should call a doctor for help just in case she's injured, like.'

A year later, Maurice and his wife were sitting with Dermot and his wife at *The Kerryman* sports star awards, which were taking place in Maurice's other hotel, the Gleneagle. Dermot, sitting back with a cigar and taking it all in, turned to Maurice.

'Maurice, I'd say you have a pile of claims against your insurance because of all the people that come through this place?'

'Well, funnily enough,' Maurice began, 'this place isn't too bad but that other place, Scott's, I settled a claim there the other day, and it's still puzzling me how it happened. This American fell down the last few steps of the stairs in February last year and didn't she go and sue me. We've no idea how it happened, though, or what she was doing there.'

'Why is that?' asked Dermot, his face the picture of innocence.

'We had our suspicions that she should not have been coming down our stairs at all. You know, we actually don't think it was even our hotel she fell in!'

Next thing, Dermot burst out laughing. 'You're right, she didn't!' he said. 'Sure it wasn't your stairs she fell down at all, 'twas mine!'

'She fell in your place?'

'She fell down the stairs in the Fáilte and sure didn't I see it, so I picked her up, carried her across the road and put her sitting at the bottom of the steps over in your place. I then went and bought her a brandy, and you know, I don't think I paid for the drink either.'

Maurice was dumbfounded. I'd say the poor man didn't know whether to break down laughing or crying. 'So you have people falling in your place and I'm paying them for falling in your hotel?'

Next thing, Dermot jumped up from his seat. 'Do you know what I'll do to make it up to you, Maurice?'

'What's that?' asked Maurice.

'I'll buy you a pint, sure!' said Dermot.

A few minutes later, down Dermot arrived with the apology pint. Maurice was sipping on it for a good ten minutes, as he tried to wrap his head around the new information that had come to light. He looked at the pint, then he looked up at Dermot.

'Do you know something, Dermot? 'Tis probably the most expensive pint of Guinness that I ever drank in my life!'

A Medicinal Brandy

One morning, Dermot Callaghan went to see his GP, Dr Mangan, in Killarney. After Dr Mangan was finished reading through the test results, he said to him, 'Right, Dermot, you're doing OK, but you'll have to give up the smoking. I'd like to see you cut back on the cigars, and you'll also have to give up the Scotch. If you do that, we'll be sorted.'

Dermot listened to the doctor, took his prescription and then headed off down the town with his son Paudie. They weren't halfway down the street when, without saying a word, didn't Dermot disappear … into a pub. Sure when Paudie looked around and saw no sign of Dermot, he figured where he had gone, so he headed off for the pharmacy himself with the prescription. Dermot, meanwhile, was sitting nicely at the bar counter, calling for a brandy.

As luck would have it, who was going around collecting money for the hospital, only Dr Mangan. One of the places he called into was this particular pub in which Dermot had now taken residency. Only twenty minutes earlier, he had been advising Dermot to give up the drink, now here he was looking at Dermot sipping on one. He took one glance at the big glass of brandy sitting on the bar counter.

'Dermot! I thought I told you to give up the drink?'

'Dr Mangan, you did not!' argued Dermot back. 'You did not tell me to give up the drink, you told me to give up the Scotch. Sure this is brandy!'

Today, Dermot's sons Paudie and Niall 'Botty' run the Fáilte Hotel. Dermot's wife, Eileen, runs the restaurant. She's 82 years of age and still works every single day. Morning, noon and night, she's there serving her customers. She's like an institution in

Killarney. I actually hold my clinic across the road in Scott's Hotel every Saturday, but I also meet constituents in the Fáilte, so every weekend, about an hour before my clinic, Paudie and I have this routine whereby we meet at the front door of the Fáilte, go up the stairs to say hello to his mother Eileen and get a briefing about current affairs, and then head off for a walk around the town, chatting with locals and calling into new businesses. No matter how busy my clinic is that day, I'd say I get more information and knowledge about what's going on in Killarney during that walkabout with Paudie. The minute people see us setting off from the Fáilte, well they know it isn't off to Dunnes Stores we're going for a look around. Locals know we're off out to hear of any issues people may have so they come up to us if there's something they need to discuss. I'd say we're stopped every ten feet. They don't have to make an appointment; if they happen to be there and they see us walking along, they just come up to us. It's good for business owners in particular because they might not be able to take the time out to leave their shop on a Saturday morning to come to the clinic, so instead they catch us as we're passing and call us in for a chat.

I love to have Paudie with me on this walk because he's a great sounding board. I'd say Paudie and his father would have walked miles upon miles when canvassing for the Healy-Rae name, and it's something I will always be indebted to them for. Anyone who canvasses today knows it's no easy feat, but by God, canvassing years back was something else altogether.

I remember the late Dan Barry, a councillor from Cahersiveen, telling me a story about how he went about canvassing. When Dan first ran for the council and was canvassing for votes, he had to do so by bike. I'm telling you, that man canvassed every bit of his area on a bicycle. He went to every house in the area, and when he'd be hopping a ditch or crossing a field to get from one house to another, he'd throw the bike up on his shoulders and be on his way. He was a hardy fit man but that was still a big undertaking. Imagine suggesting to some of the young candidates of today that they canvass their area solely by bike and to just throw it up on their shoulders when they're not using it? Mother of God, the looks you'd get!

The Pope, the Pigeon and John Paul

There was a lovely man by the name of John Paul O'Brien from Flemingstown, which is just outside Annascaul near Dingle. John Paul was an auctioneer, an electrician, and a strong community man. A formidable campaigner, he was always championing the interests of the farmers. My late father had great time for John Paul. If ever my father walked into a dance hall and saw him there, he'd make a beeline for him, and every single time, he would reach out his two hands and shout, 'John Paul O'Brien!' as though it were the first time he had seen him in years.

As well as being a fierce interesting man, there's a fierce interesting story attached to John Paul. In 1979, another John Paul came to Ireland, namely Pope John Paul. One of the places he visited during his time in Ireland was Limerick Racecourse. I went to this myself along with my mother. We stayed at my sister's house the night before, and at around four in the morning we started making our way to the racecourse. I was very young at the time, but I can still remember how weird it felt that everyone was walking in the dark in complete silence. No one said a word, not even the children, all you could hear was the shuffling of feet. It was actually a bit eerie when I think back on it now.

John Paul, being a very devout man, was also up and out early, and, along with his wife Eileen, landed above in Limerick awful early in the morning. Of course you couldn't park anywhere near the racecourse that morning, you had to park miles away, and I mean miles away! A man with two good knees would have struggled with the distance; God help you if you had a bad pair!

Everyone waited hours to see Pope John Paul and when we saw the helicopter flying above, a fierce excitement began to build. Once we realised it was Pope John Paul that was inside in it, well, we were ecstatic. I don't know if that type of excitement could ever be replicated for a person. It was different back then because public figures weren't as accessible as they are now through your Twitter and your Facebook and the likes.

During the ceremony in the racecourse that day, Pope John Paul released hundreds of pigeons into the sky. A short time later as John Paul and Eileen were making the long walk back to the car, John Paul realised something was happening. There was a pigeon following him. When John Paul would stop to rest, the pigeon would stop. As soon as John Paul would take off walking again, the pigeon would take off flying. After a little bit, the pigeon got very familiar with John Paul, so much so that he landed on his shoulder. Of course, John Paul was very amused with this. So he kept on walking anyway, with his pigeon friend sitting comfortably on his shoulder, until they reached the car.

To drive from the racecourse in Limerick to Annascaul, on today's fine roads, would take around two hours. At that time, the road from Limerick to Kerry was a far inferior road, and not half as straightforward a stretch as what you'd have today. The road to Annascaul meanwhile was no great shakes either, so taking that into account, John Paul and Eileen had a long auld journey ahead of them. They weren't on the road long, however, when they realised that the pigeon was flying alongside them. Every so often, the pigeon would disappear, but they soon discovered that the reason for this was because he'd land on the roof of their car for a rest.

Eventually they arrived home in Annascaul, the pigeon still with them, of course. John Paul, being the kind-natured man that he was, decided to give the pigeon some food and water, and made him a little bed for the night. He presumed the pigeon would fly away after a short while; the pigeon, it seems had other notions! He moved in, lock, stock and barrel. Every night, John Paul would put the pigeon into the little bed he had made for him and let him out the following morning. One day, very unfortunately, didn't some sort of fowl get at the pigeon and kill him. John Paul and Eileen were terribly upset because the bird had become like a loyal pet. He hadn't left from the second he started following John Paul at the racecourse. Straight away, John Paul knew what to do. He picked up his poor pigeon, hopped in the car, and headed straight to the taxidermist. He had the pigeon stuffed and from that day onwards, he and Eileen kept the little pigeon in their house.

I had been aware of the story as it had been recounted in *The Kerryman* newspaper. After reading it, I, and many others I'm sure, thought it was shocking interesting that one of the pigeons that had been released by Pope John Paul would then follow a man called John Paul all the way to his home, which was over two hours away in Kerry and then stay there until he died. You know, when you think about it, it was awful weird, to be honest. I definitely think there was some religious association to it because it's almost too strange to be explained away.

Sadly, didn't John Paul himself pass away in April 2013. I was at his wake, and while there, I happened to ask what had become of John Paul's pigeon. Next thing, one of the mourners pointed to the cupboard that was near the end of the coffin, and said, 'Michael, the pigeon is never far away from John Paul.' Sure enough, there was the pigeon, standing on the press, looking directly at his friend John Paul. From 1979 onwards, that pigeon had stayed with him and here they were now, together in death as well.

Ask a Digger Driver

I will rarely, if ever, take the expected route when I'm faced with a problem. You'll know from the last book that when I'm sick, it's not a doctor I'll make an appointment with, but a vet. Well, whenever I need advice on a political matter, the phone number I'll dial will never be that of a political consultant or some so-called expert. No, I tend to source my guidance and second opinions from those nearest to me. My father was the same. He always had a great team around him. Good, decent, hardworking people that he could call on when he wanted feedback.

I always like to call on someone like Paudie Callaghan, but more often than not, when I want to gauge the public mood on a matter, I'll usually call four or five digger drivers. There's a specific few I always reach out to. Whenever I speak with them, I know it's not just their opinions I'm getting but the opinions of thousands and thousands of people. Now, I know you're thinking, 'Is this man raving?', but let me explain what I mean.

People who drive machinery on a daily basis are a very special breed. While they're working hard, they're also usually listening to a lot of talk radio and absorbing what's being said, whether they're aware of it or not. They tune from one talk show to another; they're listening to the callers who are speaking on air, the texts that come in from the listeners, and the discussions between the host and the interviewee, and as a result, they have a good feel for what people are thinking when it comes to a topical matter. When I ask a digger driver for their opinion, I'm getting the mood of thousands of others because the person I'm asking is the one that's tuned into what the thousands are saying. I'm telling you, if you want a broad-minded opinion and a good spectrum of what people are thinking at a certain time on a certain issue, just ask the driver of a digger, lorry or tractor.

One for the Road

Sometimes, even the most loyal of people have their limits; that cut-off point where they stop and say, 'Ah now hang on here a minute, you're taking the p...'

Well, I remember the day I nearly pushed poor Paudie Callaghan to his limit. I phoned Paudie and asked him if he would meet me at the front door of a particular house in Killarney as I had to drop off a package to the woman who lived there.

'No problem, Mike,' he said. 'What sort of package is it?'

'Just a bag with a few bottles inside,' I explained.

'Bottles? What kind of bottles?'

'Arah not much, just a couple of bottles of poitín.'

'Sorry now, Mike, will you say that there again? I don't think I heard you right the first time.'

The polite way of describing Paudie's reaction would be to say he was not keen to go anywhere near the bag and its contents, but in fairness to him, he still met me at the house as arranged. The reason for the peculiar delivery was part of a promise I had made. As part of my plant hire work, I had demolished this woman's house and shop a couple of years earlier as she was putting up a new building. During the work, she asked me if I would be able to find her a bottle of poitín. I promised her I would but for some reason it completely went out of my head and sure a couple of years had passed before I delivered on my promise, so I threw in an extra bottle as 'interest' to make up for the delay.

As soon as she saw Paudie and myself at the door, we were invited inside. As we stepped into the hallway, we noticed two very well-dressed gentlemen standing in the sitting room. Bag of poitín still in hand, I greeted them but didn't know who they were. I noticed Paudie suddenly looking awful anxious though; he had the gimp of someone who was a bit uncomfortable. I also noticed the two men looking suspiciously at the bag of clinking bottles.

The woman brought us into the kitchen where I gave her the bag and apologised for taking so long to get it to her. Well she was thrilled with the bag. As we left a few minutes later, I'd say Paudie was nearly white.

'Do you know who those two men were?' he said to me.

'Not a clue. Who were they?' I asked.

'Solicitors! And one of them is the son of a judge!'

There I was practically waving a bag of poitín at the hierarchy of the judiciary and not a care in the world to be had.

No Need for Bells and Whistles

Any time a Healy-Rae is going for election, the canvass card remains the same. All down through the years, they have all been of the same style; nothing fancy, just a small card with the Healy-Rae name on it and the message to Vote No. 1. In my father's time, the cards started out in black and white, but as colour printing became more the norm, a little green and gold was introduced. Nowadays, even with all the personalisations and the likes, we still like to keep our cards simple and straightforward. No need for bells and whistles.

I canvassed for my father, my brother, my nephew, my niece and myself, but canvassing for my own son Jackie was very unusual altogether. The first day his canvass cards arrived, I saw the heading, 'Vote No.1 Healy-Rae, Jackie,' with his picture alongside it, and you know, I'd say I gave nearly ten minutes staring at it. I must have handed out tens of thousands of canvas cards for the original Jackie Healy-Rae and here was history repeating itself with the new generation.

I wasn't the only one to notice this. After Jackie had been elected, a very nice elderly man rang me to say how delighted he was to hear the news. 'Did he tell you about the night he canvassed me?' he asked. The truth was, I hadn't heard about it, as Jackie had canvassed thousands upon thousands of people in the run-up to the election. He did exactly what I had done back in 1999; he made sure he canvassed every single door himself. Even if the two of us were canvassing in an estate together, he refused to opt for the usual routine of splitting it half and half; he was adamant he wanted to go to every door himself. He was so determined about it that I didn't even try to argue with him.

Anyway, this man went on to tell me how he had been inside in his house one day when the doorbell rang. Who was it only my Jackie. This man didn't know Jackie, however, so when Jackie shook his hand, introduced himself, and handed him his canvass card, the man was taken aback. He was so taken aback, in fact, that he burst into tears. He said to me over the phone, 'When your son came to my door, said his name was Jackie Healy-Rae, and then handed me his canvass card with his name on it, I burst out crying. I did, because I gave weeks and months during elections canvassing with your father. Your father was a young man at the time, as was I. Now, here I am, an old man, and the next Jackie Healy-Rae, a young man, is canvassing at my door.'

He added, 'I couldn't answer him; I couldn't speak when I saw the canvass card.'

Of course that's when it dawned on me that the canvass card Jackie had handed this man would have been the exact same that he himself would have been handing out for my father all those years ago.

Jackie had an excellent team of people around him; a young, fresh, vibrant crew. Tradition is hugely important to all of us, however, and we felt it was imperative that we would have the more experienced canvassers, people like Dan McCarthy from Milltown, and Richie McAuliffe and Seamus Brien from Gneeveguilla and Tady Walsh from Killarney. All are great local characters who are also highly respected, and who would have canvassed for my father. When Richie got into the car with Jackie, the first thing he said to him was, 'Right, off we go, and just one thing now, Jackie. I have been doing this since 1974 and remember one thing, we never lost an election yet!'

It was as much to say, 'Jackie, don't you be the one to go letting me down!'

John Donoghue from Farranfore was another valuable canvasser Jackie had on the team. A lifelong friend and organiser for my father and myself, he had canvassed for us in every election and here he was again, this time canvassing with the Jackie Healy-Rae of the new generation. It meant a lot to see people like Dan, Richie, Seamus, Tady, John and all the others out with Jackie. It was like another tradition being carried on.

Jackie had been determined to do things the traditional way from the start. Now, in saying that, he had his own way of doing things in his campaign, things that I myself might not necessarily have done, but he did the time-honoured things like canvassing every house himself and standing on a box outside the church making speeches after mass. A lot of people might consider that outdated, but that didn't bother him one bit. It was the Healy-Rae way of fighting an election and it meant a lot to me that he wanted to continue it.

Councillor Really-Hae

I swear to God, some people are so charismatic and likeable, they'd be able to convince anyone of anything. Danny Kissane was one such person. Danny was a councillor up until I got elected in 1999 as he had retired after giving great service to the people of County Kerry. Now Danny was a real politician. Even though he ran under the flag of Fine Gael and worked as a Fine Gael councillor, people of all political persuasions would promptly tick the box beside Danny's name when they were placing their vote come election time. They didn't care what party he was with; they all voted for him because they liked him. He was so well-liked in fact that I honestly think you could have put any brand on his back and people would have voted for him.

I remember when Danny was chairman of the council, the Fine Gaelers always thought they would get special preference from Danny when it came to speaking time, what with him being one of their own, but that wasn't the case. Whenever my father wanted to voice a point at a council meeting, he had a specific way of attracting Danny's attention and my God it never failed him. He would jump up, point his hand at Danny and roar, 'Chairman! Chairman! Chairman!'

As sure as I'm writing this book, Danny would stretch out his two hands and shout back, 'Order! Order! Let Councillor Really-Hae speak!' With all the commotion going on, his tongue would get knotted and Healy-Rae would become Really-Hae.

Danny was an interesting man and no better one for a yarn or two. I remember him telling me one night how back in the 1970s he was allocated £160 for his expenses for the year. My own father would have been given around the same. People often forget that up until 1999, councillors didn't get a wage, just a small amount for expenses. These were people who gave a lifetime of service to local politics; these were real politicians who were dedicated to their communities and to helping people. People like Danny Kissane, Tommy Cahill, Pat Finnegan and Mary O'Donoghue, mother of former minister John O'Donoghue, were the kind of people I classified as 'real politicians'.

Every upcoming politician might be gunning to get into national government, but if they don't respect the work of local government then they have damn all understanding of politics in Ireland. These people gave great service. They started off rural development, sewerage schemes, group water schemes, they laid the foundations for the modernisation of our state, and I have no problem in saying that any person who underestimates their contribution is a complete and utter fool.

Arah for God's Sake, Guard!

I deliberated over whether or not to tell this story. What happened in it would be very much frowned upon by today's standards, but sure look, I'll tell it to you anyway and if you want to kick up, well the politician in question, whom I won't name, has since gone to his eternal reward so I'm not sure how far you'll get by reporting him.

My father and I were great friends with this politician; he was old school, a great country character. 'Tisn't bored you'd be with him. What you need to know here is that back when he was on the council, all council-related meetings were held in the Ashe Memorial Hall at the bottom of Denny Street, a street which for years had a two-way system for cars. Whenever there would be a break from the council meeting, the done thing at that time was for the councillors to head over to one of the nearby hotels for lunch and maybe a few drinks. On occasion, though, a few of the councillors would be slightly worse for wear upon their return.

Denny Street, anyway, was eventually turned into a one-way system, which was all well and good, but in the days after it had been made one-way, a council meeting was scheduled. Our politician friend was in attendance, but during the break, he'd had one too many with lunch. Sure when he was driving out the gate, didn't he forget the one-way system in place and off he went in the wrong direction. He wasn't thirty seconds gone up the street when a local garda spotted him and waved at him to stop. Naturally the garda informed the man that he would have to turn around and go back as the street was now one-way. What do you think the politician's response was? He got into a big fit of laughing and said, 'Arah sure for God's sake guard, do you think you'll make a fool out of me? I'm going up and down this road before you ever came here and if you think you'll ever stop me from driving up and down this road again, well you must be coddin' yourself. Now will you let me go on there like a good man!' And off he went on his journey and by God was no law enforcement going to stop him.

Now before you go bombarding the Garda Ombudsman with letters, bear in mind that this took place over fifty years ago, so don't be going getting excited with all sorts of notions that this kind of thing is considered to be acceptable behaviour here in Kerry.

Taking the Roof Over Your Car

If ever you thought a politician's life was all cushy comforts and glamour, well I can assure you, you're wrong, but if you still don't believe me, then this next story might leave you inclined to think differently! This is what I would call a prime example of the highs and lows of politics.

When John O'Donoghue was appointed to a junior minister position by Charlie Haughey, he was given a driver but had to provide his own car. When Albert Reynolds took over as taoiseach, however, what did he do only get rid of John as minister. One night not long after John had been demoted to the backbench, we were on the train down from Dublin. Now I wasn't a TD or anything like that, but I had been at a political meeting and John and I were travelling together. My car was in Kerry, but we had arranged to get off at the Mallow station, and then John would give me a lift to my car. I remember it was pouring rain at the time, and when I sat into the passenger seat of his car, I noticed there were drops of water falling from the roof and bouncing off the handbrake between the two of us. 'In the honour of God, John,' I said to him, 'how's the rain getting in?' John went on to explain that when he had been made a junior minister, they installed a phone in his car.

Now this was before technology went mobile, so to have a phone installed in your car, you had to also have a phone aerial on the roof. They drilled a hole in the roof of John's car, connected the aerial to the roof, and then installed the phone itself. When he was demoted to the position of backbencher and the ministerial job taken from him, they not only withdrew the services of the driver, they also took away the car phone, the radio, and the aerial from the roof of his car. In their haste to remove everything, they did such a bad job of patching the hole they had originally created for the aerial that water was able to drip through the roof whenever it rained.

From having a phone and a driver to being left with a hole in the roof of your car, well, if that doesn't reflect the highs and the lows of politics, I honestly don't know what does. On the upside, however, John went on to become a senior minister for many years.

A Fine Pair of Canvassers

Sometimes things can happen, whether it be on the canvass trail or just in life in general, and even though these things may leave you red-faced, sure all you can do is hope for the best, and, maybe with the help of employing a little bluff along the way, just get on with it. One day, a reporter from Radio Kerry accompanied my father and me to the village of Annascaul over near Dingle where we were set to go canvassing. It was a beautiful summer's day and the weather was scorchin' hot. It was perfect '99 cone' weather!

We parked up along the side of the street in Annascaul but as we were getting out of the car, didn't two ladies who were walking on the path across the way shout over at us to get our attention. Sure we saluted them as we would anyone else, but what did one of them do only lift her top and flash us. We took no notice and carried on. Sure a flash of a boob on a street in Annascaul never killed anyone yet.

The reporter from Radio Kerry was gobsmacked. 'Michael, Jackie, what was that all about?'

'Sure I don't know!' I said.

'Does that happen often?' she asked.

The truthful answer, of course, is that it never happened before and it has never happened since, but what answer do you think my father gave her?

'Arah that happens almost every day!' he said.

'Sure we're always getting that kind of reaction,' I added.

The poor woman got the land of her life trying to picture us being flashed by all these women on the canvass trail.

Thou Shalt not Waste Time

I'll never understand why some people waste time. Especially people in public office, who, God knows, have plenty of things to be doing. The gas thing is, when something needs doing, the people wasting time are always the first to say they have no time. I remember when a number of us were involved in serious government formation talks. We all had to be in Dublin for 9am. Those of us who were travelling from way down the country had all arrived in good time, only to be told that the meeting had been put back by an hour due to fog on the road.

'Which road?' we asked.

'The M50,' we were told.

Enda, Leo, and the rest of them were all held up. Myself, Paudie Callaghan and Risteard O'Lionaird had left south Kerry at four in the morning; Michael Collins, who was travelling from further afield – West Cork – would have left earlier than us; Kevin 'Boxer' Moran travelled from Athlone … and all of us were there on time, but yet the lads who were living ten miles away were all late and needed an extra hour. Eventually Leo arrived in, eating a yoghurt and some other healthy concoction. Enda wasn't too long after that.

The meeting went on all day and as we were wrapping up that evening, the then taoiseach, Enda Kenny, stood up and announced, 'Right, we'll meet here again at ten o'clock in the morning.'

I piped up. 'Hold on a second there, taoiseach. What's this "starting at ten o'clock" nonsense about?'

'How do you mean, Michael?' asked Enda.

'What's wrong with you, Taoiseach?' I said. 'Why are we starting at ten o'clock in the morning when we could start at seven? If we were to start at seven, look at the power of work we'd have done by the time ten o'clock came around!'

The one man who baulked was Leo. He wanted to start at 10am.

I turned to Enda again. 'Can't ye get up on time and be here for the meeting at seven o'clock? And Leo will have time for his yoghurt too.'

They pushed for 9am instead, but in the end, we compromised and agreed on 8am. It was the best we were going to get from them. Maybe it's a rural thing, but to me, the only way to get things done is to get up early and go to bed late. Our grandparents, great-grandparents and all the greats that went before them would have all been naturally early risers, and I can't for the life of me understand why that's no longer the case with people in general.

When government talks are taking place, the environment is high-pressured, and when you're in that environment for long periods at a time, it's the small unnecessary annoyances that rile you no end. I remember being involved in intense government talks. Myself, my brother Danny, my sister Rosemary and our lifelong friend and trusted adviser, Risteard O'Lionaird, were in the Sycamore Room with Enda Kenny, Simon Coveney and Leo Varadkar. Lunchtime arrived so we all headed into the next room for a bite to eat. The hours were long, and everyone was famished. What do you think they had arranged for lunch? Only finger sandwiches. I looked at Enda and then I looked at Danny.

'Enda,' I said. 'I'm sorry but we need real food.' We headed out and went to get a proper dinner.

The next day Simon Coveney came into us and apologised.

'Lads, we were to have outside catering coming in. The problem is we've put out the tender and we're still waiting for three of the candidates to come back with prices.'

Here we are in seriously important government talks and they're making a song and dance with their tenders and candidates over who would should provide lunch. All everyone wanted was something hot to eat.

Risteard O'Lionaird looked at me, 'Put out the tender? For the lunch? No wonder the country is fecked.'

He took the words right out of my mouth, to be perfectly honest.

Shoot to Kill

A rubber bullet was a savage thing, and by God I'd say an encounter with one would be a sore dose. They weren't a common part of the Kerry armoury, thank God, but around the time of the Troubles up north, one rubber bullet managed to make its way south and ended up in our family pub in Kilgarvan. To this day, we have no idea who brought it there or why. Wherever it appeared from, it was found and put hanging from the ceiling, right behind the bar. I often took it down just to feel the weight of it. Every time I examined it, I'd think, 'My God, if you were to get hit by one of those things, you'd be black and blue.' It always brought home to me the enormity of what was happening up in the north at the time. We were so far removed from the coalface of the Troubles by being so far south, and by only ever reading about it in the newspapers, that I suppose we became somewhat desensitised to it in a way. That bullet, however, brought home the stark reality. In recent years, someone relieved the pub of the bullet and I've no idea where it is now.

While my dealings with rubber bullets were confined to looking at one in the pub, I would never have been what you'd call gun-shy. I had grown up around guns, but I was always knowledgeable about gun safety as I had been given plenty of guidance on the subject during my formative years.

Whatever your opinion of guns may be, the use of guns for the protection of a person or their property is a very contentious issue. In my mind, it's a very simple matter. Let me put it to you this way: if there's somebody outside in your yard, taking something they shouldn't – maybe they're stealing your diesel, your chainsaw, or whatever it may be – well, OK, it's a disgrace and they're in the wrong, but legally you still don't have the right to fire a gun and shoot them, as tempting as it may be.

Now, if you're inside in the bed and you start to feel threatened when you hear an unwelcome individual (or individuals) roaming around your house or coming up the stairs at God knows what hour of the morning, then in my opinion, they're the ones looking for trouble. Should they leave your house with their ten miserable toes out in front of them and rigor mortis setting in, well I'd have no pity for them. The Homeowners Bill was the one thing the last government did that I welcomed because it strengthened the rights of people to defend themselves in their own homes. It was ridiculous to think that someone could break into your house and then sue the homeowner if they were injured during the break-in. Sure that's crazy stuff.

My father didn't give a flying damn about whether or not the law was on his side as a homeowner. If you were breaking into his home, I swear to God he'd use you for target practice. I remember one night when he was in the bar in Kilgarvan. A neighbour came out of her house and informed the locals standing outside that there was someone up on the roof of the pub. Of course, those outside went straight into the bar with the news that we had our very own south Kerry Spiderman scaling the roof up above us.

The news wasn't long making its way upstairs to where my father had been sleeping. Straight away, he picked up the gun and headed for the back window. It was black dark, but he could just about make out the shape of the intruder as they moved slowly along the apex of the roof. He reached for his glasses only to discover he had forgotten them. As a result, his aim wasn't at its best. He raised the gun and sure the cartridges started flying. He wasn't aiming to maim the culprit, no, he was aiming to take him out of this world and send him hurtling into the next one. It was a shoot-to-kill policy with my father. Naturally, the intruder instantly retreated from the roof, as you would if someone started firing a hail of cartridges at you.

I genuinely don't know how the culprit survived that night, and I'm not even talking about the warfare of which he was on the receiving end. I figured if the bullets didn't kill him, the roof itself would. You see, when the concrete barges were being moulded, broken glass was inserted into the concrete as a security precaution. That was the done thing at that time, but it was effective because it would prevent people from pulling themselves up on to the roof. Somehow, though, this genius still managed it. When he was making his way back down, however, he wasn't so lucky. The gardaí were called out and when they arrived, they found what I can only describe as a flood of blood. It seems the intruder got caught up in the glass as he was making his way down from the roof. Despite the amount of blood he left behind him, he was never caught.

Given that all of this commotion had taken place at the same time as the ceasefire in Northern Ireland, the big joke around Kenmare the following day was that not only had the ceasefire been broken in Kilgarvan the night before but there was a shoot-to-kill policy in place there now also!

My own experience with burglars was a little different in that I wasn't at home when they called around. Had I been there during their visit, well, I can't say for sure what my reaction would have been; I'm fairly sure, however, that I wouldn't have been too sympathetic towards their activities.

The burglary happened when I was out of the country. Now it's very seldom I leave Ireland as I hate being away, but on one occasion, I had to go with my son Kevin to Chicago to get his American citizenship. While we were over there, we got a call from my wife, Eileen, telling us the house had been burgled. I later found out that when the burglars had broken in and were making their way upstairs, they saw my picture on the wall. As soon as they saw it, they started to wonder why someone would have a picture of Michael Healy-Rae in their house. Slowly but surely, the penny dropped and they realised it was in fact my house they were trying to relieve of its contents. Fortunately, they seemed to make the decision there and then that it would be better to leave empty-handed. As they were heading back out, however, Eileen was on her way up the yard. Covering their faces, they raced down past her and made their escape.

Later that day, when the thieves were on the way home, they stopped somewhere for a drink and sure didn't they start talking about their escapades. That's how I came to learn of how the break-in unfolded. A person who knew me had overheard these 'masterminds' talking about the narrow escape they'd had in a certain house in Kilgarvan. I'm delighted to say they were caught in the end. Gardaí discovered that the gang in question had been responsible for a number of burglaries after technology showed that the same mobile phone was present during each break-in. It belonged to one of the suspected intruders and so they were immediately able to place him at the scene of each incident. The gardaí were able to identify that particular phone as having been inside my house as well as in other houses at the different times the burglaries were reported to have taken place. Thanks to the gardaí, the culprits were brought to justice and the ringleader is still residing as a guest of the state where please God he will remain for the foreseeable future.

The Bicycle

You know, Southern Health Board meetings can be dangerous things. Well they were for myself and my father anyway. The reason being, we'd always come home with something we hadn't planned on buying. After the meeting, we'd usually call into Atkins Machinery in Cork. We always loved heading in and browsing about the place, picking up a few auld bits and pieces.

One day, for instance, we went into Atkins' yard and saw a particular type of van. I remember my father saying, 'Cripes, that van would be handy.' In other words, he was saying, 'Cripes, let's get it!' To be fair, we both needed the van, so when we went to pay for it, we decided we'd go half and half as we'd both be getting a good bit of use from it. That was all well and good anyway until another Southern Health Board meeting rolled around. As we were leaving, I said to my father, 'Do you know what we must do today? We must go in and buy a bicycle.'

'Mother of God!' he said. 'What do you want a bike for?'

'Sure 'twould be handy!'

Very near the county buildings, there was a bicycle shop, so we headed in and had a look at the bikes on display. My father had started out his working life as a bicycle mechanic, so he was there examining each of them in detail, eyeing up the various types and everything from their gears to their tyres. One thing I was adamant about when I went in was that I didn't want anything fancy. I didn't want some racer bike that you'd find one of the Dunlop family up on. I wanted an ordinary but sturdy bike. We picked one out and tested it on the road. Off my father went, up the street, down the street, over the street and in and out every space he could find on the street. There was no buying it until it had passed his assessment. Sure enough, this one did, so we headed inside to buy it.

The first day I went to Dublin, I put the bike in the car to bring with me. It was handy for getting about the place quickly. If I needed to get to a particular office, I could just take the bike and be there in a matter of minutes, whereas going by foot would take too long and going by car would take even longer again thanks to Dublin traffic. Everywhere I used to go in Dublin, I would bring the bike, but of course, familiarity breeds contempt and I didn't give much consideration to its security. I had a lock and chain, but as I got to know Dublin, I thought, 'Sure this place is very safe altogether!' When I used to park the bike in the Dáil, I wouldn't bother locking it at all. I'd just leave it there along with the oil clothes that were folded up and pinned on the back of the bike behind the saddle.

The oil clothes were for wearing when it would be raining but sure the one thing about Dublin is that it rains very little. The Dubs don't get a fraction of the rain that the rest of the country gets, when by rights it should be the other way around. We should have the good weather and 'tis they that should have the rain. I swear, they get away with blue murder up in that place. The thing about oil clothes, though, is that if you don't use them, they go very hard. So there was my bike, nothing fancy about it, with these oil clothes on the back that were half cracking. There was nothing attractive about it as a potential theft so to be honest I didn't see any risk in leaving it unlocked.

The one place I would always use the bike to get to was the passport office. Self-praise is no praise but sure if you don't say something about yourself, who will? Myself, Jackie, Martina and Fiona, who work with me in the office, are experts when it comes to passports. We know the system inside out and if it's humanly possible to get a passport in a situation where you might not normally be able to, we'll do it. Nine times out of ten, on a Thursday when I'd be on my way back to Kerry, I'd have a heap of passports with me to be delivering to people. I used to travel to the passport office so much that it made more sense to use the bike rather than the car. One day in 2018, anyway, I pulled up and parked the bike by a tree outside; I went about my business and when I came out, wasn't the flippin' thing gone? I was genuinely gutted by the loss of it, but my upset had nothing to do with the monetary value of the bike and everything to do with its sentimental value. At that point, my father had left this world, and that bike was like another little memory of him as he had been with me when I bought it and had tried it out himself.

To this day, people ask me on an almost daily basis if the thief was ever caught and if I ever got the bike back. Well I did and I didn't! As soon as I realised it was gone, I reported it to the gardaí, but when I learned that on average twenty bikes get stolen in Dublin each day, I didn't hold out much hope of my bike thief being caught. Fair dues to the gardaí though, didn't they track him down and bring him before the courts. Although he admitted taking the bike, he unfortunately no longer had it in his possession as he maintained the bike had since been stolen from him. He then said something that I genuinely thought was absolutely hilarious. He made out he didn't steal the bike from me at all because the bike had been abandoned up against a tree and therefore his take on the situation was, 'Who in their right mind would leave a bike unlocked in Dublin?' In other words, it wasn't his fault he had taken the bike, but rather my fault for not having locked it. I mean honest to God, how could you not burst out laughing at that kind of criminal logic?

Christmas Clinics and Class Act Constituents

Sometimes you come across a constituent who is going through hell and yet somehow, they'll be cracking jokes and laughing like they haven't a bother in the world. I remember during one clinic, a man whom I had been dealing with regarding matters concerning his health, arrived in to have a chat with me. He had diabetes and, very unfortunately, some complications with his condition resulted in him having to have two of his toes amputated. Now I knew he'd had the operation in recent weeks but when he arrived in and sat down, what do you think was the first thing he said to me when I asked him how he was? With a big smile on his face, he remarked, 'Well, Mike, I can tell you there will be two less little piggies going to the next market!'

Those are the kind of people I love to meet. Decent people with a good sense of humour, who refuse to let things get to them. Then there are people you meet throughout life who, for no reason whatsoever, are just dour, grim-faced individuals who can't bear to see anyone else be happy or getting ahead. I honestly believe serial planning objectors are those kind of people. I know of plenty of situations in Kerry where people who are trying to build and set up a nice life for themselves have had their plans thrown askew by these serial objectors. It's not normal behaviour for someone to have twenty or thirty objections on the go with the planning authority at any one time. In my opinion, it's actually a misuse of the system. Why should some pain-in-the-backside individual in one part of Kerry be objecting to a person building a house in another part of Kerry and for no good reason other than to cause trouble and delay matters? D'you know something, it's crazy. Lives have been put on hold because of these serial objectors. They're a breed of people I honestly have no time for.

Planning issues like that come up in clinics all the time. Even back in my father's day, planning problems were a bone of contention. Health is the one topic, however, that would be raised most frequently in clinics. Should my own son Jackie still be a politician in twenty or thirty years' time, I can see him dealing with the very same issues that I'm dealing with in clinics today; issues that my own father before me would have dealt with also. Some things will never change regardless of how many years pass.

Personally, I love holding clinics. You do tend to take on each individual's problem and the stresses that go with it, but that's the nature of the job. Even before I was involved in politics in a professional capacity, I would arrange clinics for my father. When the Dáil wasn't sitting, I would get to work organising clinics all over the county so he would be able to reach as many places as possible. We might do a tour of clinics which could consist of maybe ten or fifteen nights on the trot. This would be what people would call 'holidays from the Dáil', but for us, this 'holiday time' would actually be the one of the most intensive periods work-wise because we'd be working our backsides off. That run of clinics would almost be like a campaign in itself.

Another time I used to do a big tour of clinics with my father was around Christmas. The Dáil wouldn't be sitting for two weeks so I would select ten nights and then advertise in the newspaper the different places where my father would be calling to each night so people would know in advance where to find us if they had an issue. I would have the route all figured out in advance so I would know how long it would take to get from one place to the next. Every night, we'd be in a different part of Kerry, holding clinics, listening to people's problems and trying to figure out the best way to get a solution for them. I learned an awful lot from my father during those nights.

The two of us would be hanging with the sleep but we'd remain in place taking notes until every single individual who was there to see us had been heard. People often ask, 'What is politics?' or they might ask about the difference in how the Healy-Raes do things compared to the way other politicians operate. Well, I believe the difference lies in meeting with people, listening to their problems, and above all keeping your mouth shut and your ears open for as long as possible. Once we have done that, we are in a position to go back to our elected positions and are able to take the problems from the coalface straight to the ears of those in power.

I firmly believe it's important that a politician goes to where the people are. It's not enough to hold one or two clinics in the main areas and expect people from all over the county to make the long journey to see you. You serve the public, therefore you should be the one going to them! I have a clinic, for instance, that takes place on a Saturday night in Kenmare. It's a small one; there might be six people at it, and there might only be two, but every Saturday night, I am seated and ready for that clinic regardless of how few might turn up.

It's the same when it comes to canvassing. Look at Hillary Clinton. She's a fine politician, very intelligent and capable, but she neglected certain areas when she was canvassing for the presidency. I'd liken her approach to the Healy-Raes not canvassing in places such as Bunavalla or the Inny Valley. It doesn't matter where you are, you go to the last corner of the most remote place in the most rural area. There might be one or two people living there, and sure they might be hardcore Fine Gael supporters, but you'd still go; you'd still ask them for their vote. You'd make your presence known, even if only to remind them that you're there if they need you should Fine Gael be too busy to see beyond the M50.

I think where some people fall short is that they don't adhere to the belief of helping those who can't do anything for you. In terms of politics, yes, votes are important, of course they are, but they shouldn't be the deciding factor as to whether or not you go out of your way to help someone.

I remember there was a pub called The Railway Tavern where my father and I used to hold clinics. The area was in south Kerry, but then the borders were moved, and suddenly the Tavern was considered north Kerry. This meant that the people we had been meeting there were suddenly no longer in our constituency. I told my father that I was going to keep holding a clinic there. Sure he thought I was mad wanting to carry on holding a clinic in a place that was no longer in our constituency. I remember saying to him, 'Sure lookit, we have been going there for so long; we've built up a relationship and a friendship with the people all around there, it'd be a fright to stop going there!' He saw my viewpoint and ended up agreeing with me on it.

Now, I have always believed that what goes around comes around, and sure enough, after about ten years or so, weren't the political borders between south Kerry and north Kerry removed and the two became the one again! That area was back in my constituency and the people whom I had been working for, and who had no way of voting for me previously, were now suddenly able to vote for us again. Forget deciding factors, if you just do what's right for the people, you cannot go wrong.

My late friend and right-hand man, Bernard Collins, had a very intelligent way of looking at life. He used to say, there will be the people who like you, people who hate you and people who don't care one way or another. Don't worry about the ones who don't like you and don't care. In order for people to like you, there will have to be people that dislike you. What it's all about is having enough percentage of support from the ones who do like you to carry you over the line.

The Healy-Rae Who's Running for Nothing!

During this last council election, my youngest son Kevin was helping out with canvassing for Jackie. As he was driving the campaign van down through the busy street in Castleisland, he took hold of the speakerphone. We had speakers attached to the roof of the van, and these were connected to the speakerphone for when we wanted to get the campaign message out there. Usually, though, there would be music playing on the speakers. Anyway, as they were driving, didn't Kevin decide to interrupt the music and introduce himself to the public. 'Hello everybody, my name is Kevin Healy-Rae! And I'm the Healy-Rae who's running for … NOTHING!'

There were three Healy-Raes running at the time and here was Kevin announcing that he was the Healy-Rae who wasn't running for a single thing!

Miracles in Canvassing

Sometimes, it can take more than a bit of persuasion to get some-one to vote for you. On these occasions, it could take something stronger, like a good helping of divine intervention. I remember a famous case in which a candidate who was running for a political party was out canvassing not too far from his own house one day. He bounced into the farmyard of his neighbour, expecting to find him working close by. This candidate walked the yard, repeatedly calling out the young farmer's name, but still there was no sign of the man anywhere. Next thing a bewildered-looking woman came out of the house and approached him.

'What's wrong with you?' she asked him, in a fairly cold, abrupt way.

'I was looking for your husband,' the man replied. 'Where is he? Is he gone away at all?'

Then came the woman's reply. 'No, he's not gone anywhere. He's in exactly the same position we put him in two and a half years ago. When we buried him.'

I'd say her response nearly sent the candidate into the ground alongside the man he had been looking to get the vote from. Don't forget, this candidate was a neighbour. He either didn't know the man had died, or had completely forgotten, and here he was in the yard calling in to ask him for his No. 1. I swear to God, as much as it would take a miracle for the deceased man to have voted for him, 'twould have taken an even bigger miracle for the widow to have voted for him after that!

No Science Needed

It would be fair to assume that the one thing you would need to do when looking for votes is to get out there and meet the people. Well, 99% of the time you'd be right, but the thing is, there's no exact science to canvassing, and sometimes it's the opposite approach that wins the vote. There's one candidate I know of who ran twice and adopted a polar opposite approach each time. The first time he was running, he put in a serious amount of work and effort. He went everywhere and anywhere in a bid to meet people and speak with them. That was all well and good, only instead of being drawn to him, people were drawn away from him. Sure enough, when the votes were counted, this candidate lost.

When the next election rolled around, the party behind the candidate in question somehow decided he was worth another go so they got to work and devised a very intelligent, albeit risky, strategy. They put him on the ticket, but they didn't want anyone to meet him. They were full sure that if people knew him, they wouldn't give him their vote. Their theory was that if people didn't meet him, or hear him speak, they just might vote for him. After all, a rare commodity is a good thing, as the saying goes. Usually that doesn't apply to politicians, but lo and behold, on this occasion, didn't it work! It was one of the most low-profile election campaigns I've ever seen. Usually it's key for the public to know the candidate, but in this case, it was the 'not knowing' that worked!

Something Different

Sometimes, when canvassing, you have to do something different. It's all well and good being quiet like the last candidate I was telling you about, but you know, I always think it's a much better policy to make a bit of noise.

When Castleisland was brought into our area, Mike Jack Cronin, Derry Healy and my brother Danny went up there canvassing. They'd had it arranged that they would go into a disco there. Now this particular disco was full of young people; it wasn't the most obvious place for canvassing, but rather than standing outside with canvass cards and waiting for the revellers to come out, they had decided they would head on in.

Do you think they went in quietly? Did they hell. Sure once they were inside, they had the DJ announce their arrival. What do you think the three did next only walk in with two accordions and a guitar! Danny led the trio. He walked onto the dance floor with his accordion in tow. Mike Jack was behind him with another accordion, and Derry was behind him again with his guitar. Right into the thick of the crowd they went and sure once they were on the floor, the three of them burst into a tune. The place had gone from dance to trad in a matter of seconds. I'd say anyone who was sober wouldn't have known what the hell was after happening, and God only knows what the more inebriated punters thought. Regardless, the crowd went mental for it. They absolutely loved it. It was a risk, but thankfully one that worked in their favour. There wasn't a sinner inside in the club who hadn't enjoyed the impromptu performance.

The trend of going into nightclubs canvassing was one started by Paudie Callaghan from the Fáilte. He decided that my father, who was 67 years of age at the time, should go into discos in

Killarney to meet the young people of the town. Sure most of them had never met a canvassing politician, and you can be sure they had never met one canvassing inside in a nightclub. The punters got a massive kick out of it, and my father equally enjoyed the craic of it, so with it being somewhat of a success, Paudie ended bringing him into every disco in Killarney that he could find. By going into nightclubs, they were reaching an enormous pile of young voters, many of whom would also have been first-time voters.

Now can you imagine the reaction if a politician walked into a nightclub above in Dublin and started playing an accordion? I'm telling you, that lot in Dublin are a different breed altogether.

The Comatose Canvasser

If you have never been on the canvass trail, it's hard to describe how physically tough it can be. It's enjoyable but it can, and does, take its toll on your body when you're at it for days on end. You never really get used to it, and to be honest, nothing prepares you for it. I remember when my brother Danny created an awful stir altogether. Danny went to collect our good friend and supporter, Derry Healy, as they were to go off canvassing together. Derry wasn't ready when Danny arrived, so Danny parked up for a bit. A few minutes later, Rosie, Derry's wife, ran into the house in an awful panic. 'Danny's outside in the car,' she said, 'and I think he's dead!'

It turns out she had gone out to the car to say hello to Danny but he was completely unresponsive. She became a bit concerned because it didn't look like he was just sleeping. She kept calling his name in a bid to wake him, but when she tried to move him and still got no response, well the poor woman nearly lost her own life with the fright she got. In she went screaming that Danny might be dead. Derry, hearing the commotion, tore down the stairs and ran outside, where he let out the most ferocious roar towards the car. Next thing he saw the head move. Danny was so exhausted from the canvassing that he had completely passed out. So now you know, the next time you see canvassers, offer them a strong cup of coffee!

Popularity Can Goose You

I tell people not to worry, but truth be told, I don't take my own advice. I always worry. When I was director of elections for my father, I worried about the campaign, that we might have missed an area when canvassing, or that we wouldn't get enough votes. Once my father was elected, I found a whole new batch of problems to be worrying about.

I always worried more about other people's elections. When there's a Healy-Rae on the ballot paper, all I want to do is help them as best as I can. I myself got a very good vote the last time, which I was very thankful and eternally grateful for, but the closer the next election gets, the more I can hear in my head people saying, 'Oh don't worry about Mike, sure Mike's alright, he'll get plenty of votes.' No vote is secured until it's in the ballot box.

The real test for me will be the next election. Will I get enough people to vote for me? If I do, that's great. If I don't, well I'm goosed. There's no point then in people saying, 'Oh we'd never have thought you'd lose.' I've seen extremely popular candidates lose elections in the past, and it's not because they weren't wanted, it was because constituents thought their vote wasn't needed. They give the vote to someone else because they think the other person will be fine, but sure if everyone goes in with that attitude, the candidate hasn't a hope of getting in. I can't emphasise it enough, if you don't vote for the person, they won't be there to represent you.

Dan Joe's Divilment

When I was very young, I had a fascination with Nora Quill; a great woman who lived next door to us in Kilgarvan. Well, I thought she was just mighty, and I loved calling in to see her. She was always all about me and sure I was always all about her. Any time I would go in to see her, she'd make me these beautiful scones and we'd have a cup of tea.

Now Nora was a big Fianna Fáil woman. She was devoted to the party. When Jack Lynch was on a whistle-stop tour of Kerry in 1977, Nora even got me to light a big bonfire outside on her lawn for when Jack would be passing. My father had been in charge of organising Jack's cavalcade around the Ring of Kerry so when he saw the big blaze Nora had arranged in her garden for Jack, didn't he stop the cavalcade and get Jack to step out and say hello to Nora. Well she nearly had a heart attack when she saw him walking towards her. I'd say if Pope John Paul himself had been walking alongside Jack Lynch at that moment, I doubt Nora would have even noticed! Not only did Jack share a few words with Nora, he went inside and had a cup of tea with her as well. At this point, it was as if Christmas had been brought forward especially for Nora. She was in her absolute element.

The funny thing is, the house that Jack Lynch walked into that day had actually been the scene of a village mystery ten years earlier. The presidential elections had been taking place at the time and one of the candidates in the race was Tom O'Higgins, who was running for Fine Gael. The candidate for Nora's beloved Fianna Fáil was Éamon de Valera. Early one morning, when Nora went outside, didn't she spot an enormous Fine Gael election poster for Tom O'Higgins pasted to the gable of her house. Back then, election posters were pasted onto a wall or a building, but my God were they glued. Once they were up, only God or a few months of bad weather would be capable of taking them down.

Well, when Nora saw this Fine Gael masterpiece on the side of her house, her mouth fell open and I'd say the poor woman thought she'd never again close it. Nora was a very quiet and placid woman but when she went up to the village that day, she was like thunder. She was determined to find the Fine Gael people who had the cheek to put up their party poster on the house of a devout Fianna Fáil woman. Despite her efforts, could she hell track anyone down who had even been remotely involved. Once the election was over, poor Nora was left with the Fine Gael stamp on the side of her house. It was only many years later that we discovered that the whole thing had actually been a prank on Nora, and one that was orchestrated and executed by none other than Dan Joe Quill, her own son!

Now, Dan Joe was one of the finest people that Kilgarvan ever produced; he was also one of the most entertaining people you could meet. He knew how much his mother loved Fianna Fáil so, in the mood for a bit of devilment and blaggarding one day, didn't he decide to get a Fine Gael poster and paste it to the side of the house! He wanted to see the craic that would ensue when his mother went in search of the Fine Gael culprits. I'm actually not too sure if he ever admitted it to her.

Dan Joe spent most of his life living and working in South Africa. He was based in a suburb called Three Rivers. Whenever he'd come home, he'd regale us with tales of South Africa and what life was like there. Whether these tales were a little bit exaggerated for our amusement or not, I don't know, but they never failed to entertain us. I remember him telling us one day that when he would go to bed at night, there would always be a few bodyguards standing outside his house. Sometimes the area where he was living wasn't always the safest place to be, and so bodyguards were required at times. We used to be gripped by his stories; captivated by the idea that a man would be inside in his bed while people were outside awake all night keeping watch for fear that anything would happen to him. To this day I don't know if that bodyguard story was true, but it sounded great at the time when we were young and had a small set of ears and a big head for soaking up these stories. Sadly Dan Joe never came home to Kerry to retire. He passed away in South Africa in May of 2018.

Dan Joe's relation, who was also born in Kilgarvan, was none other than Michael J Quill, a famous union man known as Red Mike. Michael J once brought New York to a standstill for three days after he formed the Transport Workers Union of America. I remember hearing about when he came home to Kilgarvan on one occasion many years back. He arrived in the village in a big white helicopter. At the time most people didn't have telephones inside in their houses, and only a few would have had cars, so it was a huge novelty when Michael J came to visit in a helicopter. I'm told he was wearing a very fancy suit and a white hat at the time. I can only assume it nearly had the same atmosphere as that of a royal visit.

Dan Joe's sister, meanwhile, is Maureen Quill, whom most of you will know through politics. Maureen left Fianna Fáil and went to the Progressive Democrats. She became a PD TD! The world is a big place and Kerry is certainly a fine big place, but I always think it's mad that one corner of a small village managed to generate four TDs – Maureen, my late father, my brother Danny and myself – not to mention a union man who brought the busiest city in the world to its knees!

Go Away With Yourself

Whether you're a politician, a retailer, a doctor, a customer service assistant, whatever the case may be, when you deal with the public on a daily basis in a professional capacity, you learn an awful lot about human nature. Ninety-nine point nine per cent of the people are nice but I still find it amazing that there are people out there who are so full of nastiness that their days are spent venting that hate on social media. Their time is taken up with writing horrible things about people they don't even know.

I spoke about the topic on the *Late Late Show*, and what I said seemed to resonate with people, because everyone with a phone has either witnessed it or experienced it. Can you imagine being such an awful character that you would write horrible things about someone? I mean, you wouldn't walk up to them and say it to their face, but you'll write it down on a permanent platform for everyone to see? The irony of the whole thing is that when someone writes a nasty comment about another person, it likely won't change the way people think about the person being targeted but what it does do is tarnish the reputation of the person writing the rubbish. It alters the way in which people would be inclined to view them. If someone I knew posted nasty comments about another person on Twitter, not alone would my opinion of them go way down, I would genuinely be embarrassed for them as well.

People who have never met a Healy-Rae might have a preconceived notion of what the Healy-Raes are really like, but if they actually met any one of us in person, they might come away with a completely different opinion. They'd find that we're not half the things they make us out to be. I remember when I made a comment that people shouldn't be worrying about things and that they should take every day as it comes. Straight away, someone was pounding out a reply online, saying something along the lines of, 'Oh that's easy for you when you're born into property and money.' That person definitely didn't know me because if they knew me, then they would know that I worked for every penny I have and borrowed every penny I needed. To this day I'm still borrowing. I was given nothing; anything I have, I worked extremely hard for, so for somebody to make that assumption just shows they didn't have a clue what they were even talking about.

If people write dirty things about you or to you on social media, take no notice and just remember that the ones doing the commenting and the blaggarding have damn all else for doing if this is how they get their kicks. The Healy-Raes get the smart remarks all the time. You'll have these eejits posting on the likes of Twitter and Facebook, staring into their phones while they volunteer their opinion to the nation about how horrible the Healy-Raes are; well, I have one thing to say to them and it's this. I go before the people in a very ordinary and honest way and I ask them if they want me to be their public representative to do their political work for them or not. Thankfully the answer I've been given to date is that they want me to be there for them. If some people think that it is proper behaviour to be abusive or just nasty, I would say to them go away and do something productive and don't mind firing e-bullets at people you don't even know.

Never Take Directions From a Kerry Man

Speaking as a Kerry man, take it from me when I say if you ask a Kerry man for directions, be prepared for a Kerry man kind of answer. I was on my way out to a house in a rural area one day when I rang a friend of mine looking for exact directions. I had a general idea of where the house was located, but I wasn't 100% sure. This was before the dawn of Eircodes, I might add. Anyway, I rang him up, told him where I was and asked how I would go about finding the house.

'Oh, you'll have no bother in the world, sure,' he said. 'As you're coming into the village, turn right. Go straight through the village and take the first turn left. You keep going on that road. Shtay going until you meet the dog lying in the middle of the road, then you turn right and sure isn't it the first house on the left.'

I was sure I had picked him up wrong on that last line.

'Would you ever repeat all that?' I asked.

'Ha? Sure Michael it couldn't be easier! As you're coming into the village, you turn right. Then you go straight through the village and take the first turn left. You keep going on that road and when you meet the dog lying in the middle of the road, take a right-hand turn and the first house you're looking for will be on the left.'

Well I was scratching my head.

'How in the name of God,' I began, 'do you know that this dog is going to be lying in the middle of the road? Is he the most obedient dog in all of Kerry or what?'

'Not at all,' he said back to me. 'Sure didn't I hit him just there with my car? About fifteen minutes ago actually. Turn right when you see him, and the house will be on your left.'

I followed his directions and sure enough there was the dog in the middle of the road. Now, I'm mad about dogs, and while thankful for the directions, I was genuinely awful upset to see what had happened to the poor animal. I couldn't leave him there. The first thing I had to do was take him off the road. As you'll know from the last book, I've buried a foot in a graveyard before, so giving the last rites to a dog wasn't too unusual a task for me.

You're on Healy-Rae Time Now

Every now and then, the smallest of stories can take on a life of their own and before you know it, they've turned into a juggernaut of a thing. I'll give you the best example I can think of. Each year, I bring out a calendar, only this year, a couple of details were amiss. November 4th was missing and there were only 29 days in June, things like that.

Look, it was a mistake, and a very genuine one, but not one you'd lose sleep over. Sure calendars are awful boring things altogether! At least the errors in this one made things interesting. To be honest, I didn't even realise the calendars contained mistakes until a newspaper reporter called me up and asked me about them. I laughed it off. 'Sure lookit,' I said, 'like life itself, my calendars are unpredictable!'

There I was anyway with a pile of calendars that were of no use to anyone, and not a clue what to do with them apart from maybe send them off to be recycled. The thing is, once one newspaper had run the story, the other media outlets got wind of it, and of course they all went with the spiel about the Healy-Raes re-writing the calendar. Before I knew it, I had people from all over the country ringing me looking for a copy of the calendar with the missing dates. I'll never forget one particular call I got. It was from a man who wanted to give the calendar to his wife.

'Michael? Would you send me a calendar, the one with the mistakes?' he asked.

'The one with the mistakes? Why would you want that?'

'I want to give it to my wife as a present for her birthday!'

Well I'd heard it all now. I reckoned this lad must be a glutton for punishment giving a calendar to his wife for her birthday, never mind one that was full of mistakes.

'Why would you want to go giving her that, man? Are you mad?'

'Well I'll tell you why! Our wedding anniversary is June 30th and sure don't I always forget it, but now I'm going to give her the calendar and tell her I have a very genuine reason for not remembering it this year. We can't celebrate it because it isn't on the calendar! I'd say I could even argue that we're not actually married because the date doesn't exist now!'

I had another man ring me. The date of his mother's birthday was missing from the calendar.

'She was going to be 95 on her next birthday,' he said to me. 'So I'm going to give her your calendar and tell her she can be 94 for another year because the date is missing from this year!'

When I was out canvassing with my son Jackie, niece Maura and nephew Johnny, I would have to bring a pile of calendars with me. I would also have to make sure they were the wrong ones because at some point along the canvass trail, I would be guaranteed to hear the words, 'Do you have a calendar, Michael? I don't want a correct calendar; I want the one with the mistakes.'

Some people wanted the calendar because they were fully convinced it would become a collector's item one day; others wanted one for no reason at all other than the fact that they had heard about the missing dates on a political calendar and thought it was a gas story altogether. I had a few people thank me for it saying they'd had a very bad day on such a day but because it wasn't on the calendar, they wrote it off as though it never existed. At this rate, I have a good mind to bring out another calendar next year with a brand-new pile of mistakes.

Well I Won't, Well I Will

Maybe it's my imagination, but I honestly think that in order to be a businessman in Kerry, you have to be smarter than a businessman anywhere else. You don't have the same resources as those in towns and cities, so from that perspective, you'd have to be a wily sort of character. When you come from a very rural area, people don't often expect you to have the smarts about you, and sure, let's be honest here, hasn't there been many a city slicker who has tried to pull the wool over the eyes of a country person.

My father always had a smart way of doing things. Rather than hiring something, he'd buy it, use it, and sure then he'd hire it out himself so he could make back the money he had originally spent on it. In life you have to be plucky and take a chance. It's very easy to sit back and say, 'Well I won't,' but it takes a gambler to come along and say, 'Well I will!'

There's one prime example I could give about the industrious nature of a Kerry person. When tenders were being accepted for the construction of the memorial building on the site of the Twin Towers, every big building contractor worth their salt pitched for it. Who do you think won the bid? A company called Navillus. And who are Navillus, you might ask? Well, only the Sullivan family from over in Ballinskelligs. Their company is their surname Sullivan spelled backwards – Navillus.

The founders – Donal, Kevin and Leonard – were young brothers who left Kerry for New York in the 1980s and created a massively successful company specialising in skyscrapers. I couldn't tell you why three young lads from rural Kerry decided to specialise in city skyscrapers, but they did, and they made a damn fine success of it too. Their sister Helen is also involved in the company now and together they have achieved an unimaginable level of success. I remember watching an awful interesting documentary about Donal, Kevin and Leonard. If you get a chance, you should watch it. They explained that when Navillus is tasked with the building of a skyscraper, they have to get a certain amount done each day otherwise the sums don't work. Kevin explained the logistics of it and the method to the construction. It was amazing to listen to them speak about the practicalities of creating sky-scrapers, but above all, to hear them speak about their beginnings and the journey to where they are today. I mean, here were lads who hadn't a fiver when starting out and now they're talking about profits that read like phone numbers.

There are so many Kerry businesspeople who have grown their businesses to an international level. They're in London, America, the Far East, but regardless of where they are in the world, they all have one thing in common. They started out with absolutely nothing and just worked and worked and worked. You go over to London and you'll find the place was built by Kerry people. The Green Murphys, for instance, left Kerry for Britain with nothing to their name and yet they went on to become massive employers in construction over there. They employ thousands. We call them the Green Murphys so as to differentiate them from another Murphy family in Kerry, Cahersiveen to be precise, who are also big employers in the UK construction industry.

Then you have another Kerry-born construction magnate, Dan Tim O'Sullivan. When Dan Tim left his native Glenbeigh, he had £5 in his pocket. He now employs over 2,000 people. People like that prove that anyone can achieve anything they set their mind to if they just put the head down and work hard.

If you want me to explain what a real Kerry entrepreneur is, it has nothing in the whole wide world to do with money. What motivates them is the 'doing' aspect. It's about being able to do things. It's about getting on. In the same way John B Keane was born to entertain and make a mark in the literary world; these people were born with business in their DNA. When you're self-employed like that, you're up against the world, and you really have to fight to make your mark. I'm telling you, if there was a survey done on the contribution to the world by people from different counties, I'm convinced Kerry would not only head the poll but blind the rest of them, although to be honest, I don't think one of my own previous business ventures would rate too highly in it.

A Business That Didn't Flower

Back in the early 1990s, when work and money were extremely scarce, nine local farmers and I teamed together and pooled our resources in a bid to break into the foliage industry. We thought this was a great idea. There was one thing we all had in common too, and that was our complete and utter lack of knowledge about foliage. Looking back, it was not a good idea to go investing money into something we knew nothing about. That didn't stop us though. Each man invested £7,500 so in the end we had £75,000. Some of us didn't even have the £7,500 to invest, but we found it anyway, however we managed it.

The business plan centred around the planting of hypericums. There are different breeds of hypericum, but the conditions in Ireland are perfect for them, so we decided to grow them and export them. That's when we made our next genius move – we decided to export them to Holland. I still don't know how we convinced ourselves that ten farmers from rural Kerry could take on the Dutch when it came to foliage.

We set up our enterprise and started growing the hypericums. We would harvest them, bring them to a shed, prune them, and then divide them into bunches before packaging them for placement on the lorries. It was like going to the local mart, except instead of going to a cattle auction, the hypericums were being transported over to auctions in Holland. It was all very time-consuming, but we were sure it would pay off.

It didn't. In fact, we lost money every time we sent over a lorry load. The bigger the load we sent over, the bigger the financial loss. In hindsight, I can see exactly why we lost money. Sure if you were a savvy buyer of this produce over in Holland and you knew that the fellas selling them to you were wet behind the ears, you'd go to town on them with the price! It's no wonder we were out of pocket. We hadn't a clue what we were doing, and sure selling flowers to the Dutch is about as daft as selling football lessons to Colm Cooper. Even though we were losing thousands of pounds each time we sent over a lorry load, we had nothing else to do with the dirty horrible things except to try and sell them.

One night, the ten of us met up at the local community centre where we always held our meetings and tried to decide what our next step should be. At one point, I lost my patience and started to get cross. It was time to admit defeat.

'Look, when you're bate, you're bate,' I said. 'We're not going to get the upper hand on these fellas in Holland. I propose that we get out of the hypericum business before the hypericums put us out of business.'

We had to be good-humoured about it and take our beating. Trying to keep the venture afloat in the hopes of things turning around in our favour was just madness at that stage so the only thing left to do was plough the hypericums into the ground and take a 100% loss. Despite the frustration of a business going bust, I do honestly believe we learn more from our failures than our successes. Well, once I had learned my lesson from the experience, I put it out of my mind and didn't think of it again. That was until I found myself sitting opposite King Willem-Alexander and Queen Maxima of the Netherlands. It was a state event and I was there on behalf of the European Union Affairs Committee. The purpose of the meeting was to engage in a serious discussion about matters such as Brexit, the Irish diaspora in the Netherlands and, likewise, the Dutch living here in Ireland.

As we were finishing up, we started chatting about Sneem, a place that is very special to King Willem-Alexander as he had spent time holidaying there as a child with his parents. He had also brought his wife, Queen Maxima, to Sneem some years ago in a bid to relive what he had seen as a child. Somehow, I doubt himself and Queen Maxima participated in the 'wife-carrying competition' while they were there.

During our chat about rural Kerry, didn't the story about the hypericums arise. I started telling the king and queen about the venture, and to be honest with you, they were in stitches laughing at the idea of these Irish lads thinking they could sell flowers to the Dutch when the Dutch had been at it all their lives.

Whatever about hypericums, there's one business I definitely wouldn't even try to make money in, and that's music. My cousin Gerald, a jarvey and entertainer, had bought an accordion from a Dublin-based seller on Done Deal, so I agreed to meet the man outside the Dáil to pay him for the instrument and to test it out to make sure it was all in working order. As I was giving the accordion a go on the side of Kildare Street, this big black jeep pulls up beside me. Down rolls the window. Who was it only Louis Walsh.

'Michael, isn't it a shame you can't sing!' he shouted out at me, with a smile on his face.

I looked at him with feigned shock and horror on my face.

'Mother of God, who said I couldn't sing?' I asked

The poor man's expression dropped. He got in a desperate fluster thinking he had caused me some offence, which was an awful surprise altogether because Louis Walsh is the last person you'd think would give a flying damn about causing offence.

'Oh God sorry, Michael, I was sure you couldn't sing!' he said.

'Well, I'm sorry to tell you, Louis,' I began, 'you were actually right the first time. I can't sing. Not one note can I sing in fact!'

'Jesus, it's a shame you can't,' he laughed, 'because if you could, there'd be money in it for the two of us!'

Do you know something, as bad as my singing is, that man is such a genius, he'd still probably find a way to make money out of that and a lot less!

Donkey Dealing

Long ago, there used to be piles of donkeys straying on the road. It wasn't that they were suffering because they had plenty of grass along the long acre, as it was called. The only thing that might have needed a bit of attention was their shoes, but a good Samaritan would usually stop if they saw a stray donkey, tie him on to something and cut his shoes to stop his hooves turning up.

We had a local man in our parish who liked to keep a few donkeys and if he could sell one or two, he would. The only obstacle in his business, however, was that donkeys didn't serve a purpose any more as tractors had taken over. They didn't have any monetary value either as anyone who wanted a donkey could easily pick up a stray from the side of the road at no cost.

This local man, however, continued to be a bit of a donkey dealer and whenever he could, he would try to sell one for a brown fiver. A fiver at the time was a big brown note, and my goodness, one of them alone would have had more value than a bundle of today's fivers. Back then we also had a red tenner, and a blue twenty pound note.

One day, anyway, the man headed for the village with a donkey he wanted to sell. He had a particular farmer in mind who he was going to approach so he headed for his house at the other side of the village. I'd say he walked a good ten miles with the donkey that day. When he reached the house, he spoke to the farmer and explained that he had a lovely black donkey for him.

'Will you buy her?' he asked.

The farmer sized him up. Now this farmer was a gentleman and didn't want to go refusing the sale because he knew how far the man had walked.

'How much do you want for her?' asked the farmer.

'I want a brown fiver,' said the man back.

The farmer had a big enough family and money would have been scarce enough for him, but he decided he would do the best he could, so he made a counter-proposal.

'What's the best you'll take?' he asked.

Sure enough, the haggling started, and by the time they were finished, the agreed figure they had reached was £3.

'There you go now,' said the farmer as he handed the man the money. 'I have no use for that donkey, so like a good man, would you ever take her away again and you can keep your £3 as well.'

As it turned out, the farmer already had enough donkeys. As the grass on his land wasn't plentiful, he didn't want the hassle of another donkey but he didn't have the heart to say no, so he had his bargaining, paid the £3 for the sale, which was a lot of money at the time, only to then inform the man that he could keep both the donkey and the money.

I always think 'tis a great pity the world doesn't have more people with as generous a soul as that farmer.

Honourably Up the Poll

Honor Crowley was a great woman, and really and truly, she was a mighty TD for south Kerry. After her husband passed away, Honor gave her life to politics and actually served as a politician right up until her own death in 1966. During her final run for the Dáil in 1965, she came out to a place called Lauragh, near Kenmare, to canvass. As part of her visit, she went into the local pub and while there, kindly stood everyone a drink. As Honor's night came to an end, however, the person who had been her right-hand man canvassing with her that day was there to see her off. You'll have to picture this, now. A bar full of people, all quiet, and what do you think Honor's man shouted out to her from the front door as she made her way to her car?

'Mrs Crowley! Mrs Crowley! The very best of good luck to you, and I hope that the next night I meet you, you will be up the pole.'

What he had meant to say was 'heading the poll', but the poor man got it completely arseways. I don't mean to be crude or to use derogatory words, but in any language there's an awful difference between being someone being up the pole and heading one! Especially when the someone in question is a 65-year-old lady.

All About Timing

Whether someone is up the pole or heading one, expressions can confuse, and I have no trouble admitting that Kerry expressions can be the most confusing of all. Coupled with a strong Kerry accent, well, all I can say is, if you're a Yank, or any nationality other than Irish, God help you in your attempts to try and follow a conversation in a Kerry pub. Your chances of success are few and far between.

I remember a good friend of mine, whom I won't name, whose young daughter was a little unwell. She was being treated at home but hadn't been getting any better, so they sought out the services of a particular doctor. One night in the pub, anyway, he was talking about the situation and how good the doctor had been. With every sentence, his voice was getting louder and more animated as he built up the story to a crescendo.

'My daughter, she was sick,' he said. ''Twas sick she was, and sicker she was getting. The doctor examined her and gave her an injection. I'll tell ye what he did for her. I'll tell ye what he did!'

Then came the roar. 'He made a man of her, so he did!'

For emphasis, he even drew a belt on the counter as he said it. What he was saying was that the doctor had cured his daughter, but I'd say his use of the term 'made a man of her' likely raised a few eyebrows from the few tourists nursing whiskeys in the corner.

One of the best expressions I ever heard came from my Uncle Dan. If you've read the first book, you'll know he was a very funny, very witty type of man. Well one evening, himself and a few others were coming home from work when they decided to have a drink in the local pub before heading on home. This was fifty years ago, mind you, so there was no notice taken then of driving with a drink or two in you. So Dan and the few lads went into the bar, and who was sitting at the counter only a certain lady who was a notorious case for what we'd call 'rising a spree', you see. In other words, she liked her drink.

Well of course, as soon as my Uncle Dan sat down, this lady started the banter, and sure you know rural country pubs, once the banter is in full swing, the drinks don't know how to stop flowing. Dan was a right character, you see; he was the best craic to be in a pub with, so while his friends were able to slip off home after one or two, Dan ended up staying much later than he had anticipated. It was the age-old story of going in for one and staying for one too many. No sooner would one drink be finished when the lady would be ordering the next round. Eventually my Uncle Dan had to insist on leaving the pub because he had to be up early the following morning for work. I don't know how he managed it, but sure enough he got up for work and my God, did he have some pain in the head. To make matters worse, he was working an older machine that wouldn't even have had a heater at the time. I'd say there was more glass missing from the windows of the machine than what was left in it. As you can imagine, one of the men he was working with started rising him about the late session with the lady in the pub.

'Well, do you know something, Dan,' said one of the lads. 'They say she'd drink the Shannon, that one.'

Despite the hungover head on him, Dan was still quick as a flash and came out with one of the best lines I've ever heard. 'Oh she would; by God she would ... she'd drink the Shannon alright ... and every tributary flowing into it!'

You have to feel sorry for the Americans when they come here. Not alone do we use phrases and words that bear absolutely no resemblance to the standard versions, I'd say our sense of humour has them puzzled at the best of times. Throw a strong accent and a deadpan sense of black humour into the mix and I'd say some Yanks are left in a permanent state of confusion over what we're actually saying.

I remember one occasion when myself and my good friend the late Arthur Lenihan were on the way to a clinic in Dingle. In the middle of the road, I spotted a dead cat, which was a pity because it seemed like it had been a fine big cat. As we drove past it, though, we realised it wasn't a cat at all, so I turned the car around and drove back to where it was. I pulled up beside it, opened the door, picked it up … and threw it up on Arthur's lap. Poor man nearly jumped through the windscreen with the land he got. It wasn't roadkill, but a woman's handbag.

'Open it up there,' I said to Arthur, 'and we'll see if there's any kind of ID inside.'

Arthur opened it up and sure there was everything and anything inside in the bag. Not the kitchen sink, but the whole bloody kitchen. We managed to find a purse within the bag, and inside this, there was an American passport and an all-merciful wad of notes. Arthur opened up another compartment of the purse and there was another cash wedge, this time in dollars.

He looked over at me. 'Mother of God, this one will be keen to get her bag back.'

I went on the phone to the gardaí in Dingle and let them know to get in touch with me if an American tourist phoned about a missing handbag. We tried to think what else we could do. We pulled in and had another look, something that would tell us more about her and where we'd be able to locate her. Sure enough, we came across a scrap of paper on which presumably the handbag owner had written the names of a hotel in Dublin, a hotel in Limerick and a guesthouse in Dingle. This was obviously her itinerary, so I phoned the guesthouse in Dingle and asked if she was there. She wasn't, they said, but as luck would have it, wasn't she was booked in for that night!

'When she arrives,' I said, 'she'll be in an awful state because she has lost everything, her bag, her cards, the lot, but tell her not to worry and not to go cancelling the cards as I have it all. Everything she has, I have it and I'll call by with it after I finish the clinics tonight.'

Arthur was tasked with minding the bag, and by God no one was going to get near it with Arthur as its security. That night, we called by the guesthouse to drop off the bag. A few people were outside at the time and sure enough as I got out of the car holding the bag, a girl came running towards me, looking beyond relieved.

We had a great chat and as I was leaving, she opened her purse.

'I must give you some money as a thank you for bringing it back to me.'

'Oh God no, you're grand,' I said, 'don't be worrying about that at all.'

We headed back to the car, happy to have done our bit for Irish hospitality, when next thing I decided to pull some Irish humour on her. Sure most Yanks take our jokes far too seriously so I turned around and said, 'Well actually, there is something you can do for me.'

She went to open the bag. 'So you will take some money?' she asked.

'No, nothing as straightforward as that,' I replied, 'but I was just thinking, would you like to marry me?'

I looked at her with the most deadpan expression I could manage. She looked back at me, and God love her, for a second, I'd say she thought I was deadly serious, never mind the fact that I was already married. Of course Arthur was the leveller in every situation and next thing all you could hear was him roaring behind me, 'Jesus Christ, would you ever get into the car, man, and don't be raving!'

Now I know you're wondering how her handbag came to be in the middle of the road. I asked her the same question myself because I couldn't fathom it. It turns out they stopped to take some photographs at a beautiful location and when she took her camera out of her bag, didn't she place the bag on the roof and quite simply forgot about it. As they were driving along, they hit a bump on the road, and sure enough the bag fell off the roof and landed where it did. As luck would have it, I seemed to be the first car to come upon it.

I'm telling you, everything in life is about timing. Unless you're telling a joke to a Yank, in which case even the best of timing won't save you because they won't understand what you're saying in the first place!

When the Wife Is on Your Back

There's only one place in the country where a man would actively encourage his wife to get on his back, and that place is Sneem. This only happens once a year, mind you, and it's always at the Sneem Family Festival. This festival is famous for its competitions, the wife-carrying contest being one of its more famed attractions. This contest required the husband to run full belt through an obstacle course with his better half up on his back, although to be honest, nobody gave a damn if it was his own wife or the neighbour's wife he was carrying. If I'm not mistaken, I think they had an egg-swallowing competition there also.

I don't know if festivals are a big Kerry thing, or just a big thing in Kerry, but what I do know is that we make a damn fine job of them. The Rose of Tralee is the one you all know about, but the events I'm talking about are the smaller village festivals. The ones that draw a crowd year after year solely because they're quirky, clever, or just an absolute joy to attend.

Take, for instance, the oyster-swallowing competition that's held in Ballylongford, out near Ballybunion. Each year they hold this contest, and for six years in a row my good friend, the former senator Dan Kiely, was the reigning champion. He was a miracle at it. Dan's record was swallowing around sixty oysters in a minute. Would you believe he ended up becoming temporarily allergic to them? Dan was actually the founder of the Ballybunion Bachelor Festival, an event that was bigger than the Rose of Tralee at one stage.

There's a pile of quirky contests and festivals like the few I've mentioned, but those sort of events are sadly on the decline as the one problem being faced by communities when it comes to

'Any hope of a vote, please?' (*Courtesy of Don MacMonagle*)

Your Usual, Bertha? You'll see many a strange and unusual occurrence in a rural pub, but I'd say the Blackwater Tavern in Blackwater Bridge is probably the only place where you'd have seen a cow sipping a pint of Guinness at the bar counter. The cow, Big Bertha, was believed to have been the oldest in Ireland, so Joe Duffy arrived down to report on the milestone for the *Gay Byrne Show*. A big celebration was held for Bertha and sure naturally, she was even brought into the pub where she was stood a complimentary pint. 'Twas only right too. (*Courtesy of Don MacMonagle*)

Walking on Water Created by photographer Don MacMonagle, this image was aptly named, 'Walking on Water'. Don asked my father to stand on two stones in the lake, but thanks to the clever angle Don shot from, you can't see the stones at all. (*Courtesy of Don MacMonagle*)

Sermon on the Mount The credit for the creation of this brilliant shot goes entirely to the photographer, Don MacMonagle. It was taken back in 1997. We had been out canvassing when Don phoned us. We were outside Sneem at the time, and he asked if we could meet him at a certain location as he had a specific shot he wanted to get. Don had it all planned out in his head, and would you believe, he even had a name in mind for the picture before the picture itself had even been taken. Don told us he was going to call it the 'Sermon on the Mount'. Looking at it, you'd swear my father was preaching his prophecy to a thousand people. The truth is, there was no one there at all! (*Courtesy of Don MacMonagle*)

Cripes, That Was Close Good God, Tom, watch your back! My father standing behind Fianna Fáil's Tom Fleming after narrowly defeating him in the election for the seat in South Kerry. (*Courtesy of Don MacMonagle*)

On the Ledge of Glory The night my father first got elected back in 1997, there were thousands of people in Killarney – the whole town came to a standstill. My father wanted to thank everyone for coming out, but the only trouble was there was nowhere he could make a speech. We were in the Fáilte Hotel at the time, so our friend and Fáilte owner, Dermot Callaghan, suggested that he and my father go out the top window with a megaphone. There was a ledge outside the window in question, but it was fierce narrow. The two men had to be minded because their safety could not be guaranteed unless somebody was holding on to them from behind, so that's exactly what Dermot's son Paudie and I decided to do. I stayed inside the window, put my hands inside my father's belt, and held on to him. Paudie did the same. As you can see from the photo, the two of them are standing on a tiny ledge, not a care in the world as they wave at the thousands of people below. Meanwhile, Paudie and I are sweating buckets worried that one of them would trip and fall … and take us with them! (*Courtesy of Don MacMonagle*)

Our Lady of the HiAce There I am canvassing Our Lady herself! This is a favourite picture of mine. We were in Dingle, canvassing for the general election, when I stuck my head in through the open window of the passenger side of Richie William's van to say hello. Whatever way I looked at the lady in the passenger seat when I first leaned in, I got an awful land. It was actually a statue of the Virgin Mary, with her seatbelt on as well, mind you. Wasn't the man in the van moving it for the nuns! I thought it was hilarious but who do you think was behind me capturing the lot on camera only Dominic Walsh? Sure Dominic is like God himself, he's everywhere. (*Courtesy of Dominic Walsh*)

Shoot for the Stars I would never have been what you'd call gun-shy. I had grown up around them, but I was always knowledgeable about gun safety as I had been given plenty of guidance during my formative years. (*Courtesy of Don MacMonagle*)

Keep an Eye on that Young Lad, Jackie! I always remember my father telling me about the late Dan Spring and the one favour Dan asked of him before he retired from the council chamber. The day in question was as much of a happy occasion as it was a sad one. Dan was retiring, but a fine tall young lad was making his debut. His name was Dick Spring, Dan's son. Before he left, Dan put his hand on my father's shoulder. Nodding over at Dick, he said, 'Jackie, will you ever keep an eye on that young lad for me, will you?' My father said he would and, sure enough, he stayed true to his word and kept an eye on Dick all throughout his time there, not that he needed to, mind you, as Dick was very intelligent and quick to learn the ropes. It didn't take him long to learn the workings of local democracy inside out. As we know, he went on to successfully climb the political ladder by first becoming a TD, then a minister and eventually a tánaiste; the only tánaiste that Kerry ever had, too. It's funny how things come full circle. Years later, when my father was on a train to Kerry, he took a bad turn and collapsed. Who do you think called an ambulance and 'kept an eye on him' until the ambulance arrived at the station? Only 'the young lad' himself, Dick Spring! (*Courtesy of Don MacMonagle*)

The Poster Trail Come election time, there isn't anywhere you wouldn't find a Healy-Rae poster, and they'll be put up by young and old! I love these two contrasting photos of my father and my son Kevin. (*Courtesy of Don MacMonagle*)

Feeling Chipper Why just eat the chips when you can eat the carton as well? Himself promoting the idea of an edible chip carton! (*Courtesy of Don MacMonagle*)

Dialling the Dáil The Nokia 6610 was always my father's phone. The mobile was everything to him, but he never graduated to the iPhone generation. He was old-fashioned and preferred buttons over touchscreen. If you were driving behind him, you'd always know if he was on the phone as the car would start to slow down and then veer slightly towards the ditch before being swiftly steered back into place. If he were around now, I don't know how he'd cope with the phone ban on the road. (*Courtesy of Don MacMonagle*)

In God We Trust It has almost become the done thing to show a lack of respect to the Church and to applaud its loss of authority, but I'll be honest, I don't entirely agree with that mindset. There was a certain period in Irish life where, when it came to getting things done, having a good priest looking after a parish could be more advantageous than having even the taoiseach himself living locally. (*Courtesy of Don MacMonagle*)

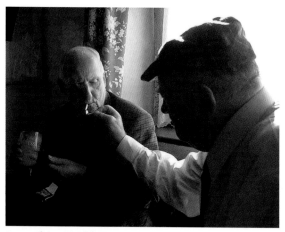

Something You'd Never See Nowadays Here's my father lighting up a cigarette inside in the pub for our neighbour and good friend, Tom Gill. You might remember Tom's name from the story 'A Tom Gill Egg!' Well this is the man himself enjoying a cigarette in the bar, a sight you would never see nowadays. (*Courtesy of Don MacMonagle*)

A Lesson in Loyalty Maurice Galvin is an example in loyalty. Everywhere my father went on the political trail, Maurice was by his side. I'll never forget the day my father was elected to the Dáil. I was in the public gallery; Maurice was sitting alongside me. As my father was making his maiden speech, Maurice was leaning forward, taking in every word. After my father had finished, Maurice sat back in his seat. As he did, I heard him say to himself, 'I don't give a damn now if I drop dead this minute!' In other words, he got to see my father be elected to the Dáil, and that was all he wanted in life. How do you beat that for loyal support? This photo was taken on the day I was made mayor of Kerry in 2002. The moment we left the council building, the first thing my father had on the to-do list was to call in to see Maurice. (*Courtesy of Don MacMonagle*)

Amazing Grace A gifted comic and actor whom we lost far too soon was the beloved Brendan Grace. I always enjoyed Brendan's comedy and found him to be so genuine and warm. Whether you were eight years of age or eighty, you could go to a Brendan Grace gig and enjoy every bit of it.

Mother and Son I was always very inspired by my mother. She was so intelligent and always had a great sense of what the future would bring. (*Courtesy of Don MacMonagle*)

No Need for Bells and Whistles Our canvas cards, as you can see, were simple and straightforward. Nothing fancy about them, just a loud and clear message to vote for Healy-Rae. Sure, even the horse in the street got the message! (*Courtesy of Don MacMonagle*)

CO. COUNCIL ELECTIONS
IND. FIANNA FÁIL

Vote No. 1
HEALY-RAE
JACKIE

I have the Experience and the Track Record

INDEPENDENT CANDIDATE FOR THE 2019 LOCAL ELECTIONS.

VOTE NO.1
HEALY-RAE
JACKIE

"A vote for Jackie Healy-Rae is a vote for hard work & common sense"

Healy-Rae: The Next Generation 2019 saw the emergence of a new generation of Healy-Raes. This was a very proud moment for the whole family.

156 Years Between Us! Here I am with my good friend Michael O'Connor in the Oaks Hotel at the annual Christmas party for the Active Retired. Would you believe he had to stop driving there recently? Sure lookit, as I said to him myself, when you're 104 years of age, there's going to be things you have to give up.

Hypericums and Royal Highnesses Discussing hypericums and business hiccups with the Royal Highnesses of the Netherlands, King Willem-Alexander and Queen Máxima.

Give a Man a Comb ... Make Sure He's Got Hair to Use it On! Would
you believe I was once sent a comb as a Christmas present? I remember
thinking at the time that the person who sent it must have been out of their
minds when they chose it as a gift for me! Barely a scrap of hair on my
head and here I was with this fancy looking comb and not a blessed thing
to do with it ... unless I took a notion to combing the hair on my chest.
(*Courtesy of Don MacMonagle*)

Telling Tales by the Fireside There's nothing better than taking time to listen to stories by a big open fire, the kind my Nana Rae used for boiling spuds or making the best apple tarts in Ireland. A good chat can do wonders, sure didn't Jesus himself tell Martha that listening's the only thing needed! (*Courtesy of Don MacMonagle*)

holding events these days is insurance and public liability. The whole country has gone shtone mad about suing. Communities have lost a lot of innocent activities over concerns of being sued should someone claim to have been hurt. Community groups struggle to secure public liability insurance, and those that do face exorbitant costs. After all, if one person takes a tumble, it's likely their first reaction will be to look for who they can sue.

I remember when I was a child taking part in a competition where you would have to get up on a greasy pole. You'd then try to belt the person next to you with a pillow or a bag of hay with a view to knocking them off, and sure they'd be doing the same to you to try and make you fall. Whoever lost their balance would slip off and land on the deck. You wouldn't have a hope of seeing that take place in this day and age.

Would you believe, even non-official activities have been stopped for fear of repercussions. During the Listowel Races, local children used to paddle in the river and when race-goers were crossing the bridge above on their way into Listowel, the children, who would be holding a pan or a bucket of sorts, would call out to the passers-by to throw them down some loose change. I remember they always used to chant 'Could you throw me down something please?' It was a great tradition, and a perfectly harmless one, but that too was stopped.

Another activity which used to be a massive deal in Kerry but has sadly declined over the years is the tug of war. Tugs of war were taken very seriously throughout the county. As I mentioned in the previous book, when my father and my Uncle Dan were on two opposing teams in a tug of war, there was a bit of controversy over which team had won and whether it was a fair pull or not. As true as God, they didn't speak for a month.

My Uncle Dan was a great one for the tug of war as he had a bit of weight on and would have been a very solid, robust man. I have great memories of watching him take on the role of anchor. He'd have the rope tied around his waist and when the competition was on, he would throw himself down on the rope. I'm telling you one thing, if Dan Rae was stretched out at the end of a rope and holding back with all his strength, you'd have a fair job ahead of you in trying to pull him forward, not to mind all the lads in front of him as well.

When it came to a tug of war, the hardcore participants were so dedicated to it, they would have left their guts on the field behind them before they'd give in. One of these was Big Mick Sweeney from Clonkeen. Big Mick Sweeney was a fierce man altogether. You could tie him on to anything and he'd pull it around the country, not a bother to him. He was a great man to have as the anchor in a tug of war; a mighty addition to a team.

I remember some lads like Mick used to even wear these old-fashioned hobnail boots to help them really dig their feet into the ground. It's no exaggeration to say that an awful lot of people who gave their everything to the tugs of war back then would have physically hurt themselves to a point where they would still be paying for it to this day. At the time, people took it so seriously, they didn't care if they were causing themselves damage. It was a case of, 'if you are strong, you use your strength' and that was it.

I don't know what it is about Kerry people, but we seem to excel at the unusual. I remember reading about a Fitzmaurice man from Tralee who beat some record for lifting the heaviest weight … while lying on a bed of nails. I mean, how on earth do you even realise you have a knack for that sort of thing? 'Twouldn't be something I'd be inclined to try myself any time soon.

Karma Healy-Rae

There's 'right' and there's 'wrong', but sometimes in life, you have to be your own adjudicator of what's right and wrong, and you have to make your own call on the standards of proper and improper behaviour. I remember one time as a teenager, about seventeen or so, I carried out a fairly big painting job for a local man. He had built a new house and gave me the job of painting it, inside and out. I also had to supply the paint. I was delighted to get the work. I would do my usual job during the day and every minute I had spare in the evening, night and weekend, I would be over at this house painting.

Painting a new house is especially time-consuming because the walls tend to soak up a lot of paint. As a result, I gave many a night inside that house painting, and usually with minimal light and just a radio blaring into the early hours of the morning for company. I finished the job anyway and the result was immaculate. Everything was exactly how the person wanted it, but there was only one problem. The homeowner, to put it politely, 'forgot' about calling to me afterwards.

When you're young like that, you'd tend to be too polite when it came to payment, so I gave him the benefit of the doubt for a long time after the job had been completed. I let it go until eventually I picked up the courage to ask him for the money. I was told the money would be coming, but then even more time started to pass by and there was still no sign of it. This went on and on for about a year, and while I was cross about it, I was more disappointed than anything else that this person would do such a lousy thing.

In the end, after plenty of thought, I decided there was only one thing I could do. I knew they had a tractor, so I decided to relieve them of it. I asked my mother to bring me up to the house one day when I knew they wouldn't be there. Straight away I sat up on the tractor and headed for Kilgarvan. There were no mobile phones at that time, so as soon as I reached Kilgarvan, I parked up the tractor and phoned the garda station local to the area where I had taken the tractor from. I got speaking to a very nice garda. The best way to describe him would be to say he was a garda of great understanding! I told the guard what I was after doing; gave him my name and address and then I gave him the details of the person I had taken the tractor from. Of course the first thing the garda said back to me was, 'Why in the name of God did you take the man's tractor, and why in the name of God are you telling me, of all people?'

I told him that I had wanted to inform him of the theft before the other man did. I went on to explain to him about having been hired to paint the man's house; I had each bill in front of me and could tell him how much I myself had paid for the paint, how many days and nights I had given working for the man painting his house and how long I had been waiting for the payment promised. To cut a long conversation short, the garda's exact words to me were, 'Well I hope he comes to me to report the tractor stolen!' I knew there and then that I had the garda onside and that they were understanding of the predicament in which I had found myself.

I waited a few days and then I phoned the individual from whom I had relieved the tractor. He answered, but then there was no caller ID that time, so he wasn't afforded the opportunity to ignore my call.

'Do you know the tractor that's parked out the back of your house?' I asked.

'I do,' he said

'Well, if you check, you'll realise it's not parked there any more!'

The phone went silent for a moment.

'Why isn't it parked there?' he asked.

'Because I have it!' I informed him. 'What's more, I'm keeping it, but any time you feel like getting your tractor back, come and pay your debts to me and once I'm paid, I'll gladly give you your tractor back. Hell will freeze over before I give you back your tractor without you giving me the money you owe me.'

The man got the message and, well, let's just say hell is still hot, and the man is still without that tractor!

From the Guawl to the Ground

While I'm convinced of the smarts possessed by those who reside in the rural areas, I will be the first to admit that our enthusiasm can sometimes trump the smarts on occasion. I'll never forget my father telling me what happened when he was driving along one day and saw a neighbour, Johnny Brien, walking along the road. We would pass the Briens numerous times a week because they would often be out tending to sheep on their land which was right beside the road. My father would never dream of passing one of them without hooting the horn and waving. One day anyway, and this now was like a gas scene from D'Unbelievables, old Johnny Brien was walking along the road with a big bag of animal ration in the guawl. Now, the expression 'in the guawl' might sound a bit foreign to people outside of Kerry. What it means is, if you're holding a bag or a box up against the front of your body and your two hands are clasped around the front of it, well we'd call that 'in your guawl'.

Poor Johnny was walking along the road anyway with his bag of animal ration in the guawl, and who was driving towards him only my father. Sure of course my father started hooting the horn at him and flashing the lights like he'd always do, but what do you think Johnny did? He knew straight away it was my father's car, and without thinking, didn't he let go of the bag of animal ration and put up his two hands to wave back at my father. Down goes the bag of ration, hits the ground and bursts open in front of Johnny and my father. When I think of it now, you know, 'twas like something you'd see happen slow motion in a comedy.

Uncle Dan and Half a Tractor

At one point during his job as a digger driver, my Uncle Dan was making a road for the Department of the Forestry, as they were known at the time. One day a young recruit went off the road with his tractor and trailer, so Uncle Dan was given the job of hauling him back out. It was in a precarious enough position, so Uncle Dan had to organise the rescue, shall we say, although with the state the tractor and trailer was in, 'twas more of a recovery operation.

So anyway, Dan went down and rigged up the tractor so that it could be towed out by another one. He then hopped into the tractor and signalled to the young recruit in the other tractor to start the towing. There was Uncle Dan sitting in the cab waiting for things to get going when he realised he could see the young lad driving the tractor but there was no pull on his one; in other words, Dan and the tractor were staying put. What the young lad didn't realise was that when he went to pull Dan out, something had gone wrong and hadn't the tractor Uncle Dan was sitting split in two parts!

There was the young lad, heading off down the road happy out with half of Uncle Dan's tractor behind him. The radiator, the front axle, and the front two wheels were all gone, and Dan was left holding on to a steering wheel and not much else. Now something like this might send another man into a fit of anger or upset, but Uncle Dan was an awful easy-going man, and his reaction to the whole thing was just typical of the kind of character he was. Sure he broke his heart laughing at him being stuck with only half a tractor underneath his backside.

The following Sunday, another recovery operation was carried out, this time for the tractor. Uncle Dan told that story for years. 'And there I was sitting in the tractor and that blind donkey of a young lad pulling away, not looking behind him at all, and only pulling a half a tractor and nothing else in the whole wide world.'

Tipping the Hat

You can say I'm odd or whatever you like, but whenever I meet a priest, I will always, without fail, put my hand up to my hat and tip it to him. It's a mark of respect, and it's just a thing I always do. It has almost become the done thing now to show a lack of respect to the Church and to applaud its loss of authority, but I'll be honest, I don't entirely agree with that mindset. I think our priests carried out, and still carry out, great work. They educated people, and for the most part, they themselves were figures you could turn to in a crisis. There was, as there will always be in every walk of life, a rogue element in the priesthood – priests who were of deplorable character – but on the flip side, there were plenty of priests of upstanding character who would have carried out a lifetime of honourable work. Why throw it all out and forget about it?

I know many priests and I like every one of them. They give their hearts and souls to the job. It truly is a vocation for them. The same priests have been put through an awful lot because they were all being tarred with the one brush. The good and the decent were being judged the very same as those who committed vile acts.

I remember one particular village in Kerry where the local priest was massively popular. He was just like all the rest of us. We were inside in a pub holding a clinic one night and the local men, who were all friends of my father and myself, introduced us to this particular priest. He was there having a drink with them. I hadn't even realised he was a priest, because to look at him, well, he didn't have the gimp of a priest.

As I got to know him, I'd say he was one of the best priests I ever in my life dealt with. A real good man to get people going to mass. He'd do those short masses, and people used to love it.

Whenever there was a big GAA match on that everyone wanted to attend, what he'd do at the start of the mass was announce to the congregation that the mass would have to be 'fairly lively'. I think his way of putting it was along the lines of, 'Now ye know the shtory lads! We're all going to the same place today, so this'll have to be fairly lively.' He'd be wanting to go to the match himself, and he knew his parishioners would too, so the sermon would be brought down to literally minutes. Sure the parishioners would all be delighted.

On this night in the pub anyway, a local man was talking to myself and my father, when, jokingly, he gestured at the priest, who was sitting beside him, and said, 'Do you know what this divil did to us lately? He stopped us smoking at the back of the church!'

The priest put his pint down on the table.

'Ah sure look, Padraic, don't mind me and just think about how it would look to strangers coming into mass. Lads smoking at the back of the church wouldn't look right at all!'

I don't think there was even a smoking ban in place at the time, but the locals were used to having a cigarette or two at the back of the church. This priest was so well-liked, however, that instead of being sour at the priest, the man was instead almost lamenting not being able to have a cigarette at mass any more.

Having a parish priest who's in tune with the parish and the people is extremely important and I believe we have been fortunate in Kerry with the priests we've had. To this day, I'm grateful for all the wonderful priests we were blessed with in Kerry. People think having a minister or a TD in their area will get things done. The fact of the matter is this. There was a certain period in Irish life where, when it came to getting things done, having a good priest looking after a parish could be more advantageous than having even the taoiseach himself living locally.

I remember when we had a priest called Fr Jeremiah Dillon. When he arrived in our parish, Fr Dillon had a new school built, and he had both the community centre and the church renovated. He organised fundraisers in the community that went a long way in helping various projects get off the ground. He was honestly like a businessman in the way he would formulate and execute all these plans and goals for the community. As well as being a priest, Fr Dillon was a farmer, so he knew what other farmers were going through because he was facing the same things himself. I remember he used to have the most beautiful red setters that he would bring out hunting with him. I always admired him so much for all the good and positive things that he did. The solid work he undertook is still there to this day. People look at things like the local community centre and think it just came about by itself. It didn't. It's there because of exceptional priests like Fr Dillon who took the initiative and spearheaded the operation.

The main priest at my father's funeral was a man called Fr Kevin McNamara, the wonderful parish priest of Moyvane. We also had our own local parish priest Fr Con Buckley but as Fr Kevin was a lifelong friend of the family, we wanted him there also, and let me put it to you this way, if I were dead tomorrow morning myself, 'tis Fr Kevin I would want saying my mass too. Whenever Fr Kevin left a parish, he would be classified as a monumental loss. He was always a great man for motivating and mobilising a community. If the priesthood was an army, Fr Kevin would have the largest force behind him because all he'd have to do is put up his hand and everyone would follow him. He has that charisma and that character about him. If you go to a funeral that is officiated by Fr Kevin, he makes it so special and so personal to the deceased. It's not just another funeral, or another burial he must carry out. Before he sets foot on that altar, he will know everything about the deceased, and everything about the family. He puts time, effort and thought into it, and considering how dying is something every one of us will have to do, and the last thing we'll ever do, well you'd like to think you'll be sent on your way to meet your maker by a good man who has put some thought into your send-off!

Dr Dineen

Dead or alive, there aren't too many people in Kilgarvan that I wouldn't know of given my line of work, but if there's one individual I'd love to know more about, it's the man who was known as Dr Dineen. He wasn't a doctor, though. I remember my good friend Johnny Lucey telling me that Dr Dineen was a butcher who would kill his own sheep for meat. Not exactly a comforting fact to learn about a man known as a 'doctor', but trust me, he might as well have been a doctor as he was a mighty man for the cures.

He was the seventh son of a seventh son, and because he could cure people using just his hands, he became known as 'Dr Dineen'. Nobody in the parish ever called him by his first name; he was only ever referred to as Dr Dineen. It kills me when I think of all the people who have since left this world who would have known him and could have told me all about him had I only asked.

I do know that Dr Dineen had the ability to cure certain ailments and allergies; things that people didn't have names for at that time. Whenever people were sick, they'd go to Dr Dineen quicker than they would an actual doctor. He was always the one to go to if you had ringworm, which almost everyone back then managed to get at some stage or another. It was easy enough to pick up, as you'd get it from cows and calves. I remember my mother often talking about Dr Dineen and praising his gift. Unfortunately there was nothing written down about him during his time on this earth. No written records, no audio recordings, nothing. Even the house he lived in has taken on a new identity and is now a very popular fast food restaurant. All we really know about the wonderful Dr Dineen is that he was just an ordinary man with an extraordinary gift.

Gleann na nGealt – Valley of the Mad

Whether you believe the stories or not, there's a lot that can be learned from Irish folklore and the piseogs that are passed down from one generation to the next. Some have a good bit of truth to them, whereas others have that question mark that leaves it to the listener or the reader to decide if it's authentic.

Folklore, for instance, would tell you that before there were psychiatric hospitals or anything like that, there were caves in South Kerry's Gleann na nGealt that were said to cure people who were deemed 'mad', so to speak. Gleann na nGealt itself translates as Valley of the Mad.

If a person was considered 'mad', they would be brought to the caves, tied up and left inside for a while. This, it's believed, cured them of their madness. If I'm being honest, I think being tied up and left in a cave is what would actually drive you mad in the first place, so I can't tell you if the technique worked or not.

I do know that there's a famous well in that valley and the water within in it is said to be able to cure a variety of ailments from stomach upsets to depression. People to this day will travel from afar to drink this water. There's no religious connection to it; it just became well known as a result of the word-of-mouth stories and folklore attached to it. People who were sick, or who had someone belonging to them who was ill, would come for the water and report it having done them some good afterwards.

Around ten or fifteen years ago, a documentary was made about the well but as part of the report, the documentary makers decided to take a sample of the water for testing so they could establish whether there were any grounds for the claims surrounding its healing properties. It turns out there were! When the water was scientifically tested, it was discovered that it contained a high concentration of lithium, a chemical commonly used in the treatment of manic depression. Who knows, but maybe the moisture on the cave walls contained lithium and that's why they were believed to cure anyone left inside there for a period of time.

While people thankfully don't frequent the caves for a cure these days, the well itself is still very popular. A great woman and community activist called Brigid O'Connor, who has canvassed with me, lives near it and regularly has callers to her door looking for directions to it.

Years back, you'd hear a lot of stories about all sorts of things, but you'd never be sure where the story came from. The one thing I remember everyone taking very seriously though was the protection of lisses, or faerie forts as they were also known. A liss is a circle of trees, sometimes with a pond in the middle, though not always, but it was believed that faeries lived there. If you were working with machinery in a field where there was a liss, you wouldn't dare go near it with the machine. You'd hear horror stories of the strange and unfortunate things that happened to people who had only recently disturbed a liss, and you know, it would put the fear of God in you.

Another superstition that was around when I was young was that a Catholic could not set one foot inside a Protestant church. I've no idea why or what would happen; in fact, I don't think we were ever told, but I do remember that the warning was always issued with the inference that something bad would happen to you if you broke this rule and went into a Protestant church. Thank God there's no more nonsense like that any more. A testament to this is the time when the people of Kilgarvan used the old Protestant church for mass when our Catholic church, St Patricks, was being renovated.

A story from modern times that may one day be folklore is that of the Kerry Nessie. Not many people know this, but Kerry once came very close to having its own Loch Ness Monster. There was always talk of an 'unidentified creature' inhabiting Muckross Lake in Killarney. The lake is quite deep and sure you know yourself, deep lakes will always inspire people to believe there might be something down there. After years of such talk doing the rounds, a scientist was brought over from the states to investigate it. I actually don't know what he found but presumably it wasn't the creature they were looking for or we'd surely to God have heard something about it. I guarantee you, in years to come, it will be the stuff of folklore.

The sad thing is that so many folk stories and tales from previous generations have been taken to the grave. Thank God for people like the renowned County Clare folklorist Eddie Lenihan, who sources stories from the older generation and then relays them to the public. He's an extremely interesting man, the kind who would have you so engrossed in a story that you'd completely forget to look at your phone. 'Tisn't more apps we need, it's more of those people.

Another person I used to love listening to years ago was the late seanachaí, Eamon Kelly. One thing I used to absolutely adore was when RTÉ would have him on television telling stories at Christmas time. I remember he would always be wearing a traditional cap and an old tweed waistcoat. I used to hang on every word that would come out of his mouth. Young or old, he'd have you completely enthralled by his stories.

I'm not Really Superstitious But...

Sometimes strange things happen, and you know, they'd honestly put you thinking. The kind of things I'm talking about would be in the same vein as a 'coincidence', but they're definitely not a coincidence, because they're too strange to be just that. I'll give you an example or two and sure can't you decide for yourself!

Late one Sunday night, around one in the morning I'd say, I left Listowel and headed for Kilgarvan. I was driving behind this slow car when I decided to overtake it. I had a good bit of road ahead of me and if I stayed driving so slow behind this car, I'd only fall asleep. I overtook the car anyway, when next thing I noticed the car in question suddenly start to speed up, like the driver was trying to keep up with me. Even though the road was quiet, whenever I'd come upon a car and overtake it, the car behind me would do the very same.

Bear in mind, now, I cover a lot of road so there are few things that would strike me as strange, but this carry-on was strange enough for me to notice. I headed in the direction of Tralee, bypassed the town and made for Farranfore. Sure enough, the car was still behind me, taking every turn I took. The more it was keeping up with me, the more suspicious I was becoming.

As we were coming into Killarney, I decided I would try and shake off this car once and for all. At the last minute, I decided to turn left and drive out the Park Road. The car followed suit. I took a few more impulsive last-minute turns. The car behind me did the same. I decided then that I would drive into Pinewood Estate and park outside a house I had in there, but for whatever reason, at the very last minute again, as I was passing an estate called Ardshanavooley, I decided to instead drive in there. These were all spur-of-the-moment decisions and I have no clue what was influencing them.

When I turned into the estate, I pulled up outside a random house there. Lo and behold, who do you think also pulled up, only this time in front of me? The car that had been following me the entire time. They not only pulled into the space in front of my car, they also then backed up as if they were really trying to get as close as possible to my car. Well I couldn't understand what was going on. A woman got out of the passenger side of the car. As she was stepping out, she was looking at me with a confused expression on her face. Next thing she produced her handbag, put her hand in and started rummaging around for something.

Now had it been some big thug of a man, I would have been convinced I was about to get shot or something, because this was all so downright bizarre. When I saw it was a very elegant-looking woman, however, well it calmed me a little, so I stayed put and braced myself for what was going to be produced from the handbag. After about thirty seconds, she found what she was looking for. A key. She walked up to the front door of the house, the one I had pulled up in front of, put the key in the door and opened it. She looked down at me again, as much as to say, what is that lad doing outside my house? The car that had been driving her proceeded to pull away.

This car had stayed behind me all the way from Listowel, and of all countless roads, streets, lanes, and estates that I could have chosen each time I tried to shake off this car, I only went and took the exact route that the driver of the car behind me was intending on taking. Then to end up at the specific house they had been driving to … now can Paddy Power or someone tell me the odds of that happening?

Peculiar Things in Peculiar Places

I would be a very logically minded person, but I honestly don't believe there's a logical explanation behind every unusual occurrence. When something strange and inexplicable takes place, or if someone tells me a story of that nature, well I would by all means question the ins and outs of it; I would at least try to find some sort of explanation. Sometimes, however, there isn't an explanation to be found, and you just have to wonder if maybe there is something of a higher force involved.

I remember when two very sound, dependable men once recounted for me a type of ghostly experience they'd had, and do you know something, while the incident in question was an awful strange one, my God I'd have absolutely no reason whatsoever to disbelieve either of them. They were never the sort to come out with any kind of nonsense.

The men told me that they had been hired to paint the interior of a house, a house that had a bit of a local reputation in that it was thought to be a bit weird. There were whispers of it being haunted, but it was mainly just known as a strange kind of place. Stories like that wouldn't have bothered these two men, however, as they wouldn't have been the superstitious sort. They didn't believe in any of that kind of thing and wouldn't have paid heed to talk of hauntings and what have you.

One day, anyway, the two were painting a room upstairs in the house when one of them decided to head down to the van to get more paint. As he was passing the sitting room door, what did he see inside in the room only a massive fire burning in the fireplace. There wasn't another sinner or soul in the place aside from themselves, and the fire certainly hadn't been burning when they first arrived. In fact, the house wasn't even occupied at the time, so God only knows the last time a fire had been lit there. Straight away the man shouted at the other man to come downstairs. Sure he was equally flummoxed by the sudden appearance of this fire.

Adding to the peculiarity of the whole thing was that there was something awful unusual about the fire itself. The two men could see the fire, but the fire didn't seem to be real. The flames were blazing mad right in front of them, as clear as the room in which they were standing, but there was nothing in the fire to keep it burning; no turf, coal or timber, not a single thing. The two men left fairly rapidly and drove straight to the address of the family who owned the house they had been painting. They explained what they had seen, and the weirdness of the fire, but rather than being alarmed, the family actually reacted with little or no surprise. If anything, they looked at each other with a sort of knowing expression, almost as though they were used to that kind of bizarre occurrence taking place in that house.

After they had informed the family of what they had seen, the two men decided to return back to the house to finish the paint job. As they walked through the front door, they made straight for the living room to see if the fire was still raging. Not a sign of it. Not only had the fire disappeared, there wasn't so much as a shred of evidence in the fireplace that a fire had been ablaze there barely an hour earlier.

Now. Let ye make of that what ye will.

Are You There, Jackie?

Here's another one for you. I would defy anyone to try and explain this for me. A week or two after my father passed away, a gang of us were inside in the house of my father's partner, Kathleen Cahill. We were all lamenting about my father, talking about how it was a disaster that he was gone. Next thing Kathleen said, 'Arah 'tis a right bags altogether. Isn't it a fright that he can't say anything to us, he can't tell us where he is, he can't say if things are alright or who he's after meeting or what he's doing now.'

The next thing, not looking at anyone in particular, she said, 'God, Jackie, if only you could send us some message to let us know that you're alright, or to let us know that you're listening to us anyway!' The next thing, every single solitary light in the house went out. The television went out, everything went black. After maybe around five seconds, the lot came back on again.

I'm not superstitious but I'm open-minded, so I wanted to double check things and see if there was anything that could explain what had just happened. I left where I was sitting and went out to check the fuse box in the hall. I'm no electrician but I'm no fool either. I could see that everything in the fuse box was exactly how it should be.

We then phoned Kathleen's next door neighbours, who were also relatives of hers, and asked if their electricity had gone out for a few seconds a few minutes earlier. No, it hadn't happened to them. We phoned a few more of Kathleen's friends nearby and asked them the same question. No power outage for them either. The only place where the outage occurred was inside in Kathleen's house exactly a second or two after she had asked for some sort of a message from Jackie to let us know he was listening to us talking about him. How do you explain that? You just can't! There are some things that just don't have an explanation.

At first, the incident frightened the absolute life out of us, but the more we thought about it, the more we were reassured and even delighted by what had happened because we realised, well, he might be gone but he hasn't left us. We realised that he's still in our lives, and regardless of what religion or beliefs you might have, a realisation like that is a great comfort.

Tributes to My Father

'Fianna Fáil has made many mistakes over the years but they must be still kicking themselves for not nominating Jackie Healy-Rae to run for them in the 1997 general election. Instead, he ran as an Independent and it marked the beginning of a remarkable political family that continues today.' An Taoiseach, Leo Varadkar, 26 June 2019.

Twenty-two years to the very day he took his seat in the Dáil, and five years after he left this world, tributes were paid in Leinster House in memory of my father, Jackie Healy-Rae. We had planned to hold this a few years ago, but sure elections and all sorts interfered with the planning of it and, eventually, it reached a point where my brother Danny and I decided that if we didn't do it as soon as possible, we wouldn't be around ourselves by the time it would be done. To hear the tributes, the Healy-Rae family, along with a number of close friends, all congregated in the Dáil gallery. We were especially delighted to have in attendance with us Mary Breen, wife of the late Jimmy Breen. Jimmy, as you will remember from the hooting hearse story, was the man who was buried with Healy-Rae canvass cards in his inside pocket!

When the tributes started, I have to say, figures such as an Taoiseach Leo Varadkar, Micheál Martin, Mary Lou McDonald, Michael Lowry, Martin Ferris, Aindrias Moynihan and so on, all spoke meaningfully and from the heart. Not one of them needed notes when speaking, which might sound like a trivial thing, but I've always believed that if you have to speak with notes, then you're not speaking from the heart. Everyone who stood to say a few words about my father made their tributes so touching and personal by each recalling their own personal interactions with him. Their stories highlighted different facets of his personality, and different sides to his character.

When Deputy Micheál Martin stood up inside in the Dáil to pay tribute, one of the first things he commented on was how lyrical my father would be in his use of language. Deputy Martin reflected also on my father's unique way of capturing a person's attention. He told of an occasion when, as minister for health, he received a letter from my father regarding the development of SouthDoc, the out-of-hours GP service in Killarney. Deputy Martin admitted that it was to his regret that he hadn't kept the letter in question, as it was what he described as 'a masterpiece in itself'. The very first line of the letter had the minister hooked from the start.

Deputy Martin explained, 'Its first sentence grabbed my attention: "This is one of the most important letters you will ever read," and I was immediately captured. He described this visionary project and concluded with a great line: "If this project does not come to pass, I know that it won't be for the want of your trying." No pressure. It did come to pass and, along with CareDoc in Carlow, it ushered in a new era of 24–7 GP care across the country.'

True to form, whenever my father wanted someone's attention, he would always instinctively know the most creative way to get it.

Deputy Mary Lou McDonald was next to speak to the Dáil, and in doing so, offered a touching tribute to my father's 'trademark wit, his plain speaking, his rich melodic Kerry accent and, of course, his flat cap'.

Referencing his famous quote in which he said he represented the people who eat their dinners in the middle of the day, she added, 'While he was sometimes teased or lampooned, he was undoubtedly one of the most astute and determined political operators ever to grace the Dáil. I am sure we can all agree on this. It is not only that he represented those who eat their dinner in the middle of the day, he had their backing as well. There is no doubt the people of Kerry always had Jackie's back and I imagine in the end for him that is all that really mattered.'

During Deputy Martin Ferris's speech, he spoke about his long-standing friendship with my father, but not before touching on his expertise as a corner forward and his reputation for 'finding the back of the net with ground hurling while never damaging one daisy; he was able to take his man out of it and make sure the ball went to its destination as well.'

When I heard him say that, I had to smile. Himself would have been only delighted with that glowing review of his GAA career! Deputy Ferris went on to recall the time my father was elected back in 1997. He had actually forgotten about this particular incident until it came up during a conversation we'd had together the night before, and I thought it was lovely that he chose to recount it in the Dáil that day.

Deputy Ferris told the Dáil, 'I remember the first time Jackie was elected as a deputy in 1997. I missed out at that time. We were in the count centre. It was as though there was an ozone layer around Sinn Féin, particularly around me. All the press was there but the other political parties were miles away. They were very shy of the camera. However, the first man up to shake my hand was Jackie Healy-Rae. He had no problem with standing in front of the camera with me. That is another great memory I have of him.'

He then added, much to everyone's amusement, 'I remember when Peig the mare went missing. It was international news, not national news. Peig was Jackie's favourite mare and he was broken-hearted. At the time, like today, there was a shortage of gardaí in Kerry and they could not find the mare. Jackie rang me and said, "Martin, boy, my poor mare has gone missing. Is there any chance you would search up around north Kerry to see if you would be able to find my poor mare?" Thankfully, at the end of the day, the mare turned up.'

When it was Deputy Brendan Howlin's turn, he gave everyone a good laugh when he talked about Jackie being one of the famous four wheels. He said, 'I came across Jackie when he entered this House after the 1997 general election. We had just left government at that time and Jackie astutely negotiated with the changed political dynamic of the House and became one of the famous four wheels that supported the incoming Fianna Fáil administration. They were expensive wheels.'

Like Mary Lou before him, Deputy John Brassil also recalled my father's penchant for one-liners, giving a nod to a few of his more famous quotes, including my own personal favourite about the rats, which I wrote about in the first book.

'His quotes were legendary,' said Deputy Brassil. 'Talking about the difficulties of people who came to him, he said they were "so poor that they couldn't buy a jacket for a gooseberry".' On another occasion, he was trying to draw attention to difficulties around a dump just outside Killarney. At a council meeting he said to the county engineer that he passed the dump on his way to the meeting and had seen rats that were so big they had saluted him. The manager, trying to lessen the effect of this contribution, said he had come in by the same road and had seen no rats. That prompted a witty journalist from *The Kerryman* to write a headline in the newspaper the following week to the effect that 'Rats salute councillor but ignore county engineer.'

Deputy Thomas P. Broughan, who stood to say a few words on behalf of the independent group Independents 4 Change, commended my father's contribution to politics, 'which showed how an individual deputy could exert great influence for his beloved kingdom. He brought the spirit of Kerry to this House.'

Deputy Michael Lowry, meanwhile, put a wonderfully colourful spin on things when he described my father has having been 'from the turf-smoke and sometimes gun-smoke wing of

Charlie Haughey's Fianna Fáil Party,' before adding how 'an unwise political miscalculation set Jackie on the independent route in 1997. That was the start of a journey which has culminated in the Healy-Rae family dominating Kerry politics.'

For his personal contribution of a story, Deputy Lowry recalled the time himself and my father were called into Brian Lenihan Jnr's office where he told them in confidence what the consequences would be for the state should the government collapse.

'It should be noted that when it came to national issues Jackie acted responsibly and in the best interests of the country,' Deputy Lowry explained. 'The government of 2007, which was supposed to have been built like a battleship, with a huge inbuilt majority, gradually disintegrated. For various reasons, many members on the government side had gone to the hills. This put Jackie and me under enormous pressure and those were dangerous and difficult times. In the context of Brexit, it is opportune to remind this House that just a decade ago our republic was defenceless, our sovereignty was gone and foreign powers were in government buildings. The very structures of the state were at the edge of a cliff. It seemed sometimes to Jackie and me, and others, that the late Brian Lenihan, a man who was then feeling the chill breath of death, was the only man left standing in the gap.'

Deputy Lowry added, 'During that time of utter crisis, Brian Lenihan called Jackie and me into his office. He took us into his confidence and outlined in the starkest terms the consequences for Ireland if that government collapsed in a disorderly way. The Troika was insisting on corrective budgets and a finance bill. When Brian Lenihan was finished speaking, Jackie took my knee in a vice-like grip and said, "Mother of divine Jesus, Michael, we are going to have to go down with them." We stood firm. Many hard decisions had to be taken. There was much drama and many cliff-hanger votes. Through it all, however, Jackie held the line.'

As Deputy Lowry recalled my father gripping his knee, you know, I could honestly picture that exact scene in my head. To hear my father's Dáil colleagues and friends recall their memories of him and speak so highly about his character was something the whole family and myself will cherish.

Drama in the Dáil Toilets

On the day the family were up in Leinster House paying tribute to my father, I couldn't help but laugh at the memory of my son Kevin during one of his previous visits to the Dáil. When John O'Donoghue was elected as Ceann Comhairle, my father made a speech. Myself, himself and our good friend Risteard O'Lionaird had worked on that speech with him for hours on end that morning, but sure when my father stood up to give his speech of congratulations to John, it didn't bear even the slightest resemblance to what we had written with him only a short time earlier.

He assured John that while he was settling into his new position up in Dublin he would look after every pothole and footpath down in Bonane, Sneem, Caherdaniel, Reenard and even on Dursey Island, the homeplace of John's wife, Kate Ann. I wouldn't mind, but Dursey Island isn't even in our constituency, it's in Cork!

There was a short break in proceedings but before it was time to head back into the chamber, Risteard went into the bathroom. As he was standing there, who was beside him only John Gormley. Gormley was about to become a minster for the first time so naturally Risteard wished him the best of luck.

Next thing, a hullabaloo broke out behind them in one of the bathroom cubicles. A young fella started shouting, 'Help! Help! I'm locked in!' It was my youngest son, Kevin, who was around nine at the time. The door of the cubicle had somehow become jammed and the young lad couldn't get out! Sure Risteard recognised the voice and knew straight away who it was. Himself and Gormley tried to figure out how they'd get him out from the cubicle when next thing Gormley took off down the corridor and headed into the chamber. Well sure what I could I do but laugh when I heard that this was our soon-to-be minister's contribution to the rescue.

While Risteard continued trying to open the door, a small head suddenly appeared from under the door of the cubicle and shortly afterwards the rest of Kevin followed suit. He'd managed to wriggle his way out. Now twenty years of age, I'd like to see him try to do that again!

Will I See You at Puck?

Puck fair was, and still is, the annual pilgrimage every Kerry person makes. Going to Puck was an experience in itself but years back, it was the kind of place where a young lad would learn a thing or two about business. You'd see the dealing going on at the horse fair, people buying and selling. These people, arah for God's sake, they're so naturally good at closing deals, they could be over in Wall Street buying and selling shares. Instead of being on Wall Street selling shares in the *New York Times*, however, they're in Puck selling a small brown foal or a white horse, or a donkey, or some sort of four-legged animal.

Whenever I would go to Puck with friends, we would always try our hand at the three-card trick, our teenage selves convinced we would get the better of the card holders. It hasn't happened yet. As we got older, a trip to Puck was still the ritual. You'd end up staying out all night only to then head straight to work the following morning, no sleep, nothing.

I remember Brendan O'Carroll's daughter telling me a great story about her time at Puck. When she was a teenager, herself and friend thumbed their way from Dublin to Killarney. They brought a small tent with them and once they had reached Puck, they set up a small stand where they would braid hair for something like 50p a go. She told me that never in her teenage years had she made as much money as when she was braiding hair at Puck. Their biggest worry in fact was being relieved of their profits, so they hid the lot in every pocket and space they could find. They were making so much money that they had to change it into large notes because they ran out of space to hide the coins. That was the sort of self-education people got from Puck fair.

Very often I would go to Puck with my cousin Gerald, who is now a jarvey and entertainer. I reckon when Gerald was born, the radio must have been blaring a song or two, or someone must have been singing him into this world, because the man has a natural gift for music. When I was young, I would sometimes stay over at his house, and I remember often waking up in the middle of the night to him playing the accordion. He would just randomly decide to break into a tune on the accordion at three or four o'clock in the morning.

As a jarvey, Gerald is one of the most entertaining people you could hope to have. Funnily enough, he actually looks a lot like the late Brendan Grace. His father, Paddy, was also a jarvey and had a horse called Bobeen. Now, Gerald's father was always known as 'Hayley' as this was how most people pronounced the surname Healy at the time. I'll never forget Gerald telling me a story about another great character called Jim Grady. About a half a mile up from Kate Kearney's pub, Jim was on his way down from the Gap of Dunloe when he met Hayley and Bobeen on their way up. At the time, Hayley was carrying three ladies and one man, but the four of them weren't very well-liked around the place. Bobeen, a small horse, was starting to struggle with his load.

'Jaysus, Hayley,' said Jim. 'Bobeen is in trouble.'

'Ha? What's wrong?'

'Well he can't see behind him, but he knows he's carrying three Connie fourstones and one thorny wire.'

And with that, off Jim went, leaving Hayley as red-faced as Bobeen!

Another great character in the Gap of Dunloe was a jarvey called Jackie Coffey. Jackie would always be standing at Kate Kearney's asking people if they would like to go in the jaunting cart. He was a right salesman, as good as the lads at Puck. One day, when Gerald was about sixteen, he spent the day working with Jackie. As they were sitting outside Kate Kearney's, didn't Jackie spot a couple of American tourists walking nearby.

'Listen now, Healy boy, I'm going to get the two of these,' said Jackie to Gerald.

Of course, Jackie, in his strongest Kerry accent, shouted out, 'Howye girls, would ye like a trip in my jaunting cart?'

'Sure!' they replied, 'Where are you going to take us?'

'I'll take ye up around the Gap of Dunloe, and up the mountains to see the scenery.'

They weren't fully sold. 'What else is up there?' they asked.

'Well I'll tell you what we'll do with you so,' said Jackie. 'Why don't we take you up to see the waterfall … and we'll even show ye the water that's behind the waterfall!'

Sure enough the two customers hopped into the carriage and Jackie won his sale! How he got around the promise of showing them the water behind the waterfall, I honestly couldn't tell you, but knowing Jackie, I'm sure he bluffed more than a politician in trouble!

Who Needs Tinder When You Have Glencar?

If any young person were to ask me for advice on where they should go looking for a fine good lad or lady in Kerry, now I'm talking about the kind that would have good prospects for the long term, well it 'twouldn't be to a nightclub or the likes of Tinder or Plenty of Fish that I'd be directing them. No, I'd be sending them to Glencar. Having canvassed the place so many times over the years, I know every house, every door and every yard there, and I have to say, it's my honest opinion that some of the finest of people, men and women, have come out of Glencar. I don't know what's in the water there but the lot of them are all very grounded, intelligent people.

One of these people is the now-retired judge James O'Connor. Whenever James was holding court, he had a great ability for reading people. He would do his best to avoid giving a decent person a conviction. He recognised that in life, good people make mistakes, sometimes inadvertently, he would always try to give them the benefit of the doubt, so that they would not be hindered when it came to employment and travel opportunities. He also came from a farming background and so, whenever he was faced with a tricky situation in court between neighbours, he would employ common sense. Anyone who has seen John B Keane's *The Field* will know how emotive people can become about land. Well, James understood that, whereas those from a city background wouldn't. That made him a good, decent judge and helped him in the decisions he made each day.

I'm telling you, when an area can produce a judge with a heart as big as his brain, you know there's something in the water there.

The Driver Who Didn't Know the Brake Pedal

One time, when the young lads were around primary and secondary school age, myself and Eileen decided to bring them to Galway for a few days. I have always had great time for Galway ever since I received some of my schooling there. Now, for those of you who haven't read the first book, I should point out here that I do have two daughters, Rosie and Juliette, as well as three sons, Ian, Jackie and Kevin, but I never refer to the lot of them as my kids or my children, I always call them 'the young lads'.

Well, each evening during our stay in Galway, we would bring the young lads to a go-kart facility. Juliette, who was rigged out in her overalls, helmet and gloves, couldn't wait to get behind the wheel, but she had never driven before, so I lifted her in and explained to her how to keep the car going. I showed her the accelerator pedal and told her that she had to press on that to go forward. The instructor came along and he too showed her how to drive the go-kart. She took off, but when she did so, it was at a fierce pace altogether. She did one lap, but I noticed it was gaining speed she was. I was terrified but as I was watching her drive around the track, it occurred to me that something was radically wrong. She didn't seem to be slowing down a little when she was coming up to corners and the likes. Next thing, as she was going around one of the turns, didn't the car fail to make the turn and instead crashed through the heap of tyres that was there as a safety barrier. Sure she put a dozen of the things flying. I took off running down to see if she was alright. By the time I got there, she was out of the go-kart and laughing away at what had happened.

'Mother of God,' I said, 'what happened you at all?'

'I dunno. Sure it's very hard to go around the turns when you're going around them so fast!'

'Juliette, that's what your brake is for! That's why you should take your foot off the accelerator. To slow down when you're going around turns.'

She looked at me with an awful serious face on her.

'Look, nobody told me anything about lifting my foot up off the accelerator; nobody told me anything about a brake. All I was told was to sit in, steer, and put your foot down to the last to make it go.'

Well, I couldn't argue with her. When I thought about it, I hadn't told her anything about a brake, I just automatically assumed she knew. And God only knows why I did! Sure you should never assume someone knows everything about a thing they have never before operated in their life!

If Only I'd Had A Camera

These days, you will never hear anyone say something like, 'If only I'd had a camera when that happened!' It's one of those sayings that has become redundant due to the simple fact that everyone these days has a phone in their hand, ready to shoot. In fact, I'd go so far as to say that those types of complaints are exclusive to the parents of the 80s and 90s. We didn't have camera phones, or even landline phones for that matter, so if our kids did something funny and we wanted to share the memory with someone who wasn't there at the time, there were only two options available to us. We'd either have to recall the moment from memory and hope they'd get the humour of it, or else we'd have to grab either a disposable camera or a film camera, hope there were enough spare shots left in the 24-picture roll (or 36-picture role if you were awful fancy), snap the picture, leave the camera or the film into the shop, wait a week for the lot to be developed, then collect the photos and pray that the picture you wanted didn't come out fuzzy. If the images weren't right, well, you were goosed.

I'm not one for photos but there was one occasion in particular where I would have liked to have had a camera with me. I had come home from a meeting one night and after a while, I noticed there was no sign of our youngest lad, Kevin, who was around ten years of age at the time. I asked Eileen where he was.

'Sure he's out there in the kitchen,' she said.

I went out to the kitchen. No sign of Kevin. Oh cripes.

Straight away, I headed across the road to where we had a pig house. I don't know why, but I had a hunch to check in there. Well the picture that was before me would have been the nicest, most endearing picture you'd have ever seen – if I'd only had a camera with me. When Kevin had gone down checking on a sow that was near farrowing, he saw that she had farrowed and lying beside her was a big litter of baby pigs. You might wonder why I'm calling them baby pigs and not bainibhs; well I have no choice, I'm afraid. Sure, I can't spell bainibhs.

To ensure they'd all be warm, Kevin had turned on the red light. Next, he had set about making a nice bed of straw for them to keep them all cosy for the night. The newborns were all spotlessly clean and huddled together, and sure the sow herself was also sound asleep, but who do you think had laid down on the straw beside them? Only Kevin. You had one sow, twelve baby pigs and a young Healy-Rae all asleep under the glow of a red light on a bad wet winter's night, and do you know something, the innocence of it all looked beautiful.

At Your Most Vulnerable

Whenever I hear of a child going missing, it brings me straight back to the day it happened to myself and Eileen. There are few things more terrifying than the realisation that your child is no longer beside you and absolutely nowhere to be seen. When the young lads were kids, myself and Eileen used to try and bring them on holiday once a year. Well, one year we headed over to Portugal. We were walking along by the beach and at some point, we turned left, but our youngest, Kevin, wasn't paying any attention and continued walking straight on.

Well it wasn't long before we realised we were a man down, and my God did the panic start. I'd say the entire beach was looking for him. The whole ordeal probably only lasted a matter of minutes, but it felt like a tortuous eternity. It actually felt like it went in slow motion. Thanks to the help of the kind people on the beach that day, we found him, but every day after that, I would take a marker and on the back of his hand I would write the name of the hotel, along with my mobile phone number so that if he disappeared again, well sure at least he could be landed back to where we were staying. Mention the incident to Kevin, and straight away you'll get the response, 'Oh yeah, the time ye got rid of me over in Portugal, yeah I remember that!'

One thing I do a lot for people is assist when a family member has an accident abroad or, worse, tragically passes away. You see, every Tuesday morning, I meet with ambassadors from various parts of Europe, and over time I have come to know them all and have built up a good network of contacts that I can utilise in the event of an emergency. I'm in a good position to help a family who may have a loved one in trouble abroad, so when I am contacted about an incident, it's made a priority. I'll put it to you this way, I can basically see nothing else from between my two eyes until the matter is sorted and the family have their loved one back home with them.

When a person passes away abroad, it's a nightmare in every sense of the word. The family who travel over are already so vulnerable, but then you add to the equation that they might not be used to travelling or they might not know the place they are travelling to. There might be a language barrier and even a cultural barrier. Then of course you have the everyday stresses that come with travelling. All these things are bad enough but under intense circumstances, they are heightened by about a million. This is why I do everything I can to help a family in that situation. It happens all too often, and having been personally involved in such cases, my heart always breaks for the family in question whenever I hear on the news that an Irish person has had an accident or has sadly passed away while abroad. You honestly can't imagine what it's like to be in that situation, and I sincerely hope none of you ever will be.

Sure That's Alright So!

I'm all for changing with the times and the likes, but sometimes, just sometimes, it would be nice if certain things stayed the way they used to be. Years ago, a 'gentleman's agreement' carried the same weight as a signed contract. You wouldn't get that so much these days. When I was younger, I was always thinking about the future, trying to secure it in whatever way I could. I hadn't two pennies to rub together, but I knew how to talk the bank manager into giving me a few more pounds so I could do the things I had in mind, like buying a digger so we could take on more digger work.

One day, anyway, I was in Killarney loading dumpers but one of the lads hadn't turned up to work so it meant that myself and the other man on site had to do the work of three men. We had to draw the loads back and forth and while we were drawing the second load, I spotted a 'for sale' sign outside a house. At the time, mobile phones had just come out, so I took mine out and phoned the number of the auctioneer on the sign, John O'Sullivan. We were talking about the house, anyway, when he told me he didn't think the house in question would fit the bill of what I was looking for. He had another one on his books, however, that he felt I should go and view. The house was in Killarney, so I decided to hop in while I was passing, meet the owners, and have a look around.

I knocked on the door and a very nice couple answered, John Quinlan and his wife, Margaret, two beautiful people. God be good to the two of them, they're now both with their maker. I got talking to them but remember now, I wouldn't have been dressed too well when I arrived at their door. I was in my work clothes and had just jumped off a dumper, so I was covered in oil and grease. As I was asking a ton of questions, John was looking at me, sizing me up, I'd say. He wasn't staying silent, but he wasn't inclined to say a whole pile either. I hadn't entered politics at that point, and they had never set eyes on me before, so their hesitance to give me the grand tour was understandable. To look at it from their side, some scruffy young lad in a cap had just dropped by, without appointment, and asked to be shown around their house. To be honest, if I had been them, I'm not too sure I'd have let me in either. In fairness to them, though, they did let me in, so I asked John if he would show me the kitchen. I asked how much they wanted for the house. John gave me the figure. I looked around again and with that I said, 'Arah, sure that's alright so,' and with those words, I shook their hands and headed back to the dumper I had parked outside.

As I was leaving, I remember they were both looking at me, kind of like two people who didn't know what to make of me. Later on that night, John was speaking to a friend of his. From what I have been told, the conversation went as follows.

'Any news, John?' the friend casually asked.

'Well you know, the funny thing is, I sort of do!' said John. 'This man called into the house today, and I don't know what to make of him.'

'Who was he at all?

'Healy-Rae is his name. Michael Healy-Rae. Would you believe it, he just called by and asked if he could have a look around the house. I'm sort of confused to be honest. The estate agent hadn't mentioned he was going to be dropping by.'

The man he was talking to knew me fairly well, so he knew exactly how I operated.

'And tell me, John, did Michael buy the house?' he asked.

'Well that's what I'm confused about,' said John. 'He was only there for about five minutes.'

'That's not the point, did he buy the house?'

'I don't know.'

'Well, let me put it to you this way, did he shake hands with you when he was leaving?

'He did.'

'And by any chance,' the friend went on, 'Did he say, "sure that's alright so"?'

'Well, to be honest with you, that's exactly what he said!'

'Do you know what you'll do, John? You'll go out and take down that "for sale" sign from outside your house, because your house is sold. Healy-Rae mightn't have the money to pay for it but when the time will come, he'll have it borrowed or begged. If he's after shaking hands with you, then you don't own that house any more.'

Our mutual friend was right. I didn't have the money for it. In fact, if I punctured a tyre on the dumper that day, I wouldn't have had the price of repairing of the tyre. That should give you an indication as to the health of my finances at that point. I would always find a way around things, though, and that day I set about making sure I would have the price of the house for John. I said it in my last book, and I'll say it again, I have never not been in debt to a bank. As soon as one loan is paid off, I'm taking out another.

To tell you the way in which the world can be so unusual, after John had sold his house to me, he bought a pub in Tarbert. When I went there canvassing, who was one of the first men who had lined out to help me canvass, only John! We ended up becoming great friends, and to tell you a further twist in the tale, when my mother was living in Killarney, her neighbours were John and Margaret's son Johnny and his lovely wife, Siobhan. They were so good to my mother while she was alive, and she doted on their young children. Today, my daughter Juliette and her husband Patrick are their new neighbours. Do you know something, it's strange the way the wheel goes around.

Garda Jack

It's gas when you think back on it now, but there was a time when, if you were a young person and a uniformed garda was nearby, well if that garda happened to make eye contact with you, it would be enough to put the fear of God in you. They had this intense air of authority. It was the same with priests as well, and teachers too, now that I think about it.

Garda Jack McGrath was one such figure of authority. To me, he was what real policing was all about. He was from Clonmel but based in Killarney and my goodness was there proper order when he was on duty. Garda Jack had a great reputation in that he was a no-nonsense guard. He wouldn't have to say anything; you just wouldn't start any messing if you knew what was good for you. That said, if he saw a person stepping out of line, they'd quickly get the proverbial clip around the ear and that would be the end of it. They wouldn't step out of line again.

At the same time, there was no one friendlier or more respected in our community than Jack. I'm adamant that he saved our state tens of thousands of pounds because rather than choke up the court system by bringing every little misdemeanour in front of the judge, he sorted it out himself, and by God, the perpetrators wouldn't be in a hurry to step out of line again, I can tell you.

Jack also used to be a football trainer. My cousin Gerald, who is now a jarvey and entertainer, was on the U-16 team he trained. My God he'd make them go in hard for the ball. It separated the men from the mice. I think Gerald was only around twelve when playing on that team and although he was small, he was strong. Sure Jack would see Gerald going straight in for the ball and all you'd hear was Jack shouting, 'Jaysus Christ, there's four fellas up on top of Healy, I don't think he'll come out of this one.' Healy always came out, though!

To this day Jack is held in the highest esteem. Now retired, and still a big giant of a man, the air of authority he has would still put the fear of God through you at times! We've been fortunate in that there have been many larger-than-life characters in the gardaí that have been stationed in Kerry, but Jack McGrath will be always be the one held in the highest esteem.

A Pint of Guinness and a Pair of Wellingtons, Please

There's a famous pub in Dingle called Dick Macks, and on the gate beside this pub, there's a very famous saying that goes, 'Where is Dick Macks? Across from the church. Where is the church? Across from Dick Macks.' It's been in operation since 1899 and my God, is it some pub! It's the old sort of establishment that also has a bit of a shop within the bar so you could find yourself buying anything from a pint of Guinness to a pair of Wellingtons if the mood took you.

The pub is owned by the McDonald family and the reason it's so famous is because the interior is pretty much the same as it was back when it was a house in the 70s, with the exception, of course, of a cigarette machine! The old Stanley range is there, and when they were turning it into a pub, they didn't go knocking walls or anything like that. They just left the various rooms as they were and put a few seats and tables in them. These days, the place is one of the most popular pubs in the county and one I have often frequented myself. It's lovely to see the new generation of McDonalds running the pub now. They're even distilling their own gin within in the pub itself.

Another favourite pub of mine is Tuohy's Roughty Bar in Kenmare. The publican was the late Eamon Tuohy, and he and his late wife Anne, or Mrs Tuohy as she was always known, ran a great business. I've always said anybody can sell drink, but it takes a great person to be a real publican. The Tuohy family are what I would call real publicans. I reckon Eamon had spent roughly around 312,075 hours, and possibly more, standing behind the bar counter. Now when I say standing, I literally mean standing. He used to get up every morning, stand behind the counter serving drinks and he would stay there from morning till night, seven days a week, month after month, year after year for 57 years. The only place he would allow himself to go would be a funeral or a football match if it was local. Other than that, he would be behind the bar working. It was an amazing length of time to give to his business. The pub now is mainly run by his sons Eamon Jnr, Ciaran and Seamus.

I have to say, I always liked calling in to see the Tuohys, and while there aren't many times when I've been left stuck for words, a night in Tuohy's bar managed to do it on one occasion. This was a good few years back. A group of Killarney women were in Kenmare one Saturday night for their usual get-together. They didn't drink alcohol, but they would always meet in a place like Tuohy's and enjoy a few minerals. Anne was a great woman for chatting with the customers, and on one particular night, didn't she start talking to one of the girls in the group. Now this girl was exceptionally well-dressed; they all were, in fact, but this one was wearing a fur coat which was quite exotic. It wouldn't be every day you'd see a fur coat on someone, so over Mrs Tuohy went admiring it and talking to the girl wearing it.

I swear I'll never forget this whole sequence of events until the day I die.

'Well fair dues to you,' said Mrs Tuohy. 'You're very glamorous-looking. Isn't she very glamorous-looking, Michael?'

'Oh she is,' I said, the right one she was asking and I not having a bull's notion about anything to do with women's fashion.

But Mrs Tuohy didn't stop there. She wanted to get a better look at the whole outfit, so she turned to her, asking, 'And what kind of lovely outfit have you on underneath that beautiful coat?'

Before the girl could say or do anything, didn't Mrs Tuohy open whatever type of mechanism was keeping the coat closed. Now bear in mind, I was sitting right beside where all this was going on and sure when Mrs Tuohy opened the fur coat, what do you think she was wearing underneath? Barely a stitch on her! And who do you think got the eyeful? Only myself and Mrs Tuohy. All I could do was look up at the roof with a face on me that was now beetroot red, and let on I saw nothing, while the rest of them, including the girl herself, got into a fit of laughing.

One publican who could almost rival Eamon Tuohy's record is Mrs Mary Reilly from Reilly's Bar, which is across the road from our own bar in Kilgarvan. Mrs Reilly gave 42 years day and night working behind that bar, all the while raising her six children. They were a farming family too, so while running the bar, she would also be making dinners every day. She would have to make dinners not just for her own family but for the relatives of her husband who were living in the house, and the workers who were employed to help out on the farm. She had to make on average fourteen dinners each day. Reilly's bar would have been busy from morning to night too, as back that time, daytime drinking would have been a common occurrence. Farmers coming back from the creamery would stop in the village for a few messages and call in for couple of pints before going home. Sure of course a couple of pints would often turn into a lot of pints. Regardless of how busy she was, Mrs Reilly always had a smile on her face.

When I got chatting to her one night recently, I asked her for her secret. I asked her how she was able to spend 42 years behind the bar and keep such a positive attitude for every second of those four decades. The pub trade isn't easy and spending 42 years in it while never once complaining, well it's a feat worthy of a medal at least. What she said to me, I thought, was very interesting.

'When people come in and have a few drinks, there's one thing you have to get into your head,' she told me. 'If somebody is trying to insult you, you had to imagine they were giving you a compliment. If you can manage that, well, when a person insults you and you respond as though it were a compliment, sure Michael, you couldn't go wrong!'

Bertie and a Different Kind of Larkin

Michael Griffin, father of the junior minister Brendan Griffin, is one of life's gentlemen. As the Aghadoe Heights Hotel concierge, he gave decades of excellent service and was extremely popular, not to mention highly respected. He probably did a lot more for Kerry tourism than any minister could do.

One time a local building contractor, a sound man called Paddy Walsh, hired me to work a digger and a tractor at the Aghadoe Heights. It was a damn fine awkward job too. I had to dig out a swimming pool inside the hotel. Michael had nothing to do with the construction side of things, but he ended up becoming almost like the project manager. If the noise from the digging was becoming a little too loud or disturbing the residents at breakfast time, Michael would come out and put the hand up. That's the only signal we needed to turn off the engine and lay down tools. We wouldn't resume work until Michael returned back out and again put the hand up. I always maintained he was the real boss because he could start us and stop us whenever he wanted! He was more powerful than a garda.

Not a million miles away in Milltown, there's a great bar called Larkin's. Larkin's is so well known for its delicious food that whenever Bertie Ahern was in the area, he would always call into the bar for lunch. This was back when Bertie was in his heyday. Normally, it wouldn't matter a damn where the man would stop for a bite to eat but the thing is, the pub across the road from Larkin's was owned by a Fianna Fáil councillor and it used to cause awful ructions that the leader of the party would always choose the rival bar over the one owned by his party member! Sure this would be a source of great amusement to the locals.

When Celia Larkin, Bertie's then partner, was in the newspapers over the tribunal, Mike McCarthy, the very witty owner of Larkin's, decided to tear out a headline from the paper which read, 'Larkin used FF money to buy house.'

He proudly stuck it up on the wall, and there it still hangs to this day!

Always Have a Backup Plan

I'm not a man for the water. I don't like it, and the only time you'll probably catch me on a boat is maybe to cross from Tarbert to Killimer on the car ferry, or maybe from Cahersiveen to Knightstown in Valentia on that ferry. Aside from that, my boatfaring experiences are few and far between. You see, I decided when I was a young lad that I wouldn't be venturing back to sea in any way, shape or form. Not surprisingly, this aversion to water was prompted by an incident that occurred when myself and a friend were on the water.

We had decided in our infinite wisdom to build a raft. Now, this raft was an unusual thing in that it was a fairly sophisticated raft. A lot of time and effort had been invested in it and we didn't do things by half. We had found some barrels to help for the buoyancy, then we sourced an engine. What was actually helping to drive the raft were the makeshift 'propellers' we had put together. These were the rims of car wheels with paddles attached; there was a drive shaft going from the engine and the gearbox that was propelling these wheels going around. There was one on both sides.

One Sunday afternoon, we decided we would test out this raft out on Kenmare Bay. We headed out on the water, and as the raft was going so well, we decided to go out a little further. Of course, confidence is a mighty thing, and sure the two of us were fuelled with plenty of it by this point. We were absolutely convinced that nothing could go wrong, so we decided to head out even further again. Nothing was of any bother to us. Sure we had plenty of petrol, and not a care in the world.

We had brought along a couple of fishing lines, so we decided to spend some time catching mackerel. We thought we were the bee's knees with our mighty supply of fish. While we were fishing, however, we suddenly noticed that the raft had started going around in a circle. It didn't take long to realise what was after happening – we were after losing a wheel. There we were, miles away from dry land, and our two means of propelling the raft were the two rims of a motor car wheel, one of which had now only gone and disappeared off the axle. All the raft was capable of doing was going around in a circle. We were goosed.

We drifted aimlessly for a bit, not knowing how on earth we were going to get back. This was the pre-mobile phone era too, so a quick text wasn't going to save the day. As we were bopping along on the raft, the waves carrying us further and further out, we cursed ourselves for not having prepared a backup plan for this type of situation.

After what seemed like a lifetime, didn't we spot a person on a speed boat. It wasn't too difficult for us to catch their attention. I mean, if you had seen the state of our raft out in the middle of the water and we barely moving, well, it would have had anyone wondering what was going on. Thankfully he had a rope on board and was able to tow us the considerably long way back to shore.

That incident taught me a couple of things. First, it taught me to always have a backup plan or at the very least a solution in the event of something going haywire. Most important, it taught me that there's a reason humans don't have gills and that maybe we were born to stay on dry land after all!

Leave It With Me

There's a lot to be said for confidence, even if it's of the blind variety. Never was this more evident than the day my father went up to Dublin for government talks. Bertie had requested a meeting with him, and himself had a hunch as to why. Sure enough, when my father and an adviser called Declan Ingoldsby headed into the taoiseach's office, Bertie explained he was short of a few votes; four, I think it was. My father's response was simple. 'Bertie?' he said. 'Leave it with me!'

Down the hallway of Leinster House he went. Who should he meet only Mildred D Fox. He had been good friends with her father years back. My father explained the situation with Bertie and the votes, and sure fair play to Mildred, she said yes straight away when he asked her to come on board.

Next, he approached Donegal's Tom Gildea.

'Tom, I hear you're having a problem with the mast in Donegal.'

'I am, Jackie,' he said.

'Not to worry, I have it sorted for you.'

Now Tom had spent a year, if not two, trying to sort out a particular mast issue in Donegal so when my father casually mentioned that he had taken care of it, well, Tom was a bit taken aback to say the least.

'How did you sort that out?' he asked in astonishment.

'I have it sorted, man! I got assurance from Bertie inside in his office there.'

Sure my father had it no more sorted than the man on the moon.

'The only thing is,' my father added, 'will you sign up for the programme for government?'

That was the second vote secured. He only needed one more to go with his own vote, and he'd have the four votes Bertie needed.

Next thing he met Harry Blany. He put it to Harry and said something along the lines of 'Come on, Harry, we'll form a government.' That was Harry on board.

Bertie likely thought it would have taken my father a few hours to get the votes secured for him. Within twenty minutes, however, my father had Mildred, Tom and Harry inside in Bertie's office ready to sign.

While they were all signing, Jackie suddenly remembered what he had promised Tom about having the mast problem sorted. He turned to Bertie. 'By the way, Bertie, don't forget what I said about the mast in Donegal. That's very important like.'

Bertie was looking at him, not a clue what he was talking about, but in fairness to him, he went along with it anyway.

'Oh no problem, Jackie. That's no problem in the slightest.'

And right there and then, thanks to my father and his Kerry-born confidence, Bertie's vote problem was no more, and Tom's mast problem was finally sorted.

Well 'Tis Yourself, Padre!

For a mighty county there's a lot of the devil in it. We have places called 'the Devil's Elbow', 'the Devil's Punchbowl' ... lads I swear, at the rate we're going, the devil himself will take up residence here if we're not careful, though to be honest, I'd say Dublin would be more his spot.

Well, thankfully I can't claim to know the devil, but the one man I do have great time for is Padre Pio. I remember when Paudie Callaghan and my father were out canvassing one day, they made their way over to one particular house. As they approached the house, didn't Paudie spot a Padre Pio badge on the car parked outside.

As they were about to ring the bell, Paudie whispered to my father, 'Jackie, whatever you are, you're very, very holy.'

My father looked at him. 'What in the name of God are you on about, man? Are you losing it?'

A lovely lady came to the door and sure as soon as she saw they were canvassing out came the questions, such as, 'Are you religious, Jackie?'

'Well I believe in God, anyway,' he said. 'And I believe in right and wrong.'

Five years later, I myself was canvassing the same stretch of road with Paudie.

The same car was in the same place, and the same badge was still there also.

'Michael,' he said to me, 'you're very, very holy.'

No more than my father years before me, my response was in the same vein of confusion. 'What are you on about, man?'

'You go to mass all the time,' Paudie said.

'But sure I do go to mass all the time!' I said back to him.

'I know, but make sure the lady we're about to canvass knows it!'

'Well, alright so, if you think I should ...'

Out the lovely lady came, and what do you think was her first question? It wasn't planning or health-related; it wasn't even government-related.

'Are you religious, Michael?' she asked.

I didn't even have to look at Paudie to know he was grinning beside me.

PJ John Francis O'Sullivan

This is not a story with a quirky ending or a funny punchline. There's no twists or eccentricity, it's just a simple story about a Kilgarvan man with immeasurable courage, and whose memory I believe should be captured in print. His name was PJ John Francis O'Sullivan, son of John Francis and Mary O'Sullivan. From birth, PJ suffered with cystic fibrosis, an awful debilitating condition that mainly affects the lungs.

While most of us have a fairly regular morning routine that we generally take for granted, a CF sufferer like PJ would have to endure a morning of side effects at their worst, not to mention a time-consuming routine of multiple medications, nebulisers and trying to free himself up for the day ahead.

Now, this young man was suffering badly with CF, but despite having to endure the condition itself and all the consequences it brought with it, he was always up no later than 5am and waiting with a smile on his face when I would arrive at 6am to collect him for work. Some days he and I would be working with dumpers, other days it might be tractors. Whatever we were doing, he would always put his heart and soul into the work, and it wasn't exactly straightforward work either. Machines back then weren't as sophisticated as they are today, so you'd regularly have trouble-some occurrences, like one of the parts breaking down again and again, track machines going bogging, tracks coming off, all which involved heavy work to get going again, but even on the worst day, not one word of complaint would you hear from PJ. He would just carry on with the work.

I have never in my life met a young man with as much courage, as much grit, and as much determination as PJ John Francis. Good God, but his fight and fortitude was extraordinary. Sadly, in 2016, PJ left us for his eternal reward.

As he had always joined us each Christmas to go clay pigeon shooting, that first Christmas after we lost him, we organised a trophy and named it the PJ John Francis Perpetual Trophy for Clay Pigeon Shooting. Each Christmas morning, neighbours and friends gather together on my own farm and we all go clay pigeon shooting together for a couple of hours. It's a competition shoot and whoever wins is presented with the trophy by PJ's mother, Mary. We're on our fourth year of the competition now, but I genuinely do hope that it will become a solid Christmas tradition for locals and will continue on for many years long after myself and the rest of the founders are gone. It's such a lovely way to not only remember the wonderful man that was PJ John Francis O'Sullivan, but to ensure his name and legacy rightly live on.

When One Word Leads to Another

When you reach a certain age, you have to be fairly mindful about who you blaggard. It's all well and good not giving a damn, but sometimes, it's that 'damn' that can land in you in a spot of bother down the road if you're not careful!

One time in a small town in Kerry, there was a group of friends comprising around five or six men and they were planning a bit of a golf outing. In the organisation of this trip, they decided to hire a small bus to take them to where they were going, but didn't they make the disastrous decision to overlook a local man's minibus business in favour of hiring from someone outside the town. The man in question, who was also one of two local undertakers in the town, quickly heard about this booking and needless to say, wasn't too impressed at the idea of being snubbed.

Well, the men headed off on their golfing trip anyway, and throughout the day of course, a few beverages of the alcoholic variety were enjoyed. And sure when the trip was coming to an end, they could hardly leave without having a few more for the road. I'd say this golfing trip was more about the beverages than the birdies, somehow.

By the time they arrived back into town, the men were in high spirits so they decided to continue on the merriment in a local pub. Off they went from the bus to the bar, but as luck would have it, didn't they meet the local busman/undertaker as they were making their way up the street. The man was obviously still reeling over the whole situation and sure when one choice word led to another and then a few more, the lot of them ended up having a bit of an argy-bargy on the side of the street. All I will say is, bridges were burned, and both went their separate ways.

For the golfers, that 'way' was the local pub to which they had been headed.

In they went, but no sooner were they at the bar when who should they meet only the man who was the town's second undertaker. They began chatting with him about something or other but of course with plenty of drink comes plenty of loose talk and sure again, didn't one word lead to another and they ended up having a blazing row with this particular man. Whatever was said I don't honestly know, but it was enough for them to leave the premises. As they were walking along, however, the fresh air started to hit, and one of the men, who was a real smart man, suddenly stopped and got into a fit of laughing.

'Stop up one minute lads,' he said. 'We must be awful fools altogether.'

The rest of them were looking at him. 'Why do you say that?' one of them asked.

'Not one of us is the younger side of seventy-five! There are two undertakers in this town and in the space of one evening, we're after succeeding in falling out and having a blazing row with the two of them. Now, is that a smart move when you're the wrong side of seventy-five?'

That story is 100% true, and if there's a life lesson to be learned from it, it's this. Don't be falling out with people who are capable of burying you!

An Irish Moon

After my mother moved from America to Kerry, people would ask her questions about life in America and what the place was like. She used to marvel at these questions, but she would always take her time in answering, making sure to vividly describe the various aspects of New York life such as the subway stations that were under the city streets, the looming skyscrapers, the lanes of traffic that would occupy just one side of the road, and of course, the streets that would be teeming with people.

There was one man, though, whose question I don't think I will ever forget. He was quizzing her one day about America and asking her all sorts. My mother appreciated the fact that this man likely wouldn't have spent a night anywhere other than the house in which he was born, never mind travel to another country, so she didn't spare the detail when painting a picture for him through her stories. She answered all his questions and, my God, was he enthralled by her depiction of what life was like in the US. His eyes were wide open in wonder. He was baffled by the idea that every place over there had electricity and telephones. Out of all the information she had given him, though, he only had one straightforward question to ask, and it was one that she wouldn't in a million years have expected.

'And tell me,' he began, his eyes furrowing a little, 'what was the moon like over there?'

My mother was taken aback. 'How do you mean?'

'Well we have the moon here, but what type of moon have ye got in America?'

The person was full sure there was a different moon abroad in America. The man had comprehended everything else – from how the subways operated to the buildings that were ninety storeys high – but the only thing that was puzzling him was the moon. My mother of course explained that even though America was over three thousand miles away, the moon we could see in Kerry was the very same moon the Americans could see. Well, he thought this was absolutely ridiculous. He couldn't understand how she could think that the moon in America was the exact same moon we had in Ireland. Not only did he think she was raving, he even told her so too!

What the Future Holds

Every year for Christmas, my mother would give me a new book, and every year without fail she would always invest a great deal of thought into the kind of book she would buy for me. She wouldn't just pick up the latest bestseller or some popular title she had heard others at the bridge club talking about; no, there was always some significance as to why she would choose the book she did.

On the night of 25 December 1986, she presented me with a book called *The Art of the Deal.* It was authored by a man whose name I had honestly never heard of until that point, a New Yorker called Donald J Trump. Straight away, I opened the book, eager to see what it was all about. The cover was a striking one. It featured a photo of the author looking all sharp and business-like in a smart black coat, shirt and tie. He was posing against an impressive backdrop of Central Park.

'Who's this man at all?' I asked.

'Read it and we'll talk about it afterwards!' my mother said.

I was a voracious reader at the time, so of course I devoured the book this Donald man had written. It was all about the various deals he had carried out, the successes he had enjoyed and the lessons he had learned throughout it all. Afterwards, when chatting with my mother about it, I decided to ask her why she had chosen to give me that particular title. I hadn't known of Donald Trump, or any Trump for that matter, so I was a bit curious as to why she had bought his book for me.

'Would you tell me,' I asked, 'what is the significance in the book?'

'I might not be around for it, but you watch that man,' she said, nodding at the picture of Donald on the cover of the book. 'That man could end up running the world yet!'

I remember her words taking me by surprise because nowhere in the book had Donald expressed so much as an interest in politics. The only passing reference he made to politics was when he was talking about the rigmarole involved in dealing with governors and the likes during his application for gaming licences in Las Vegas. There was no indication that he himself would one day enter politics. If anything, the impression I got from the book was that his opinion of politicians was a fairly low one. My mother, who had also read the book, was full sure that he could end up running the world. Looking back on that night and comparing it to the way things are today, well, she was spot on.

I do believe my mother could see into the future. I really do. She seemed to know the way in which the world was going to change, decades on from then. As far back as I can remember, my mother would tell me a story about the way in which she believed the future would evolve. She always thought it was ridiculous that people would walk out of their house with a key in their hand, sit into their car and then spend God knows how long in that car as they made their way from A to B. That, she always said, was a crazy notion of transport. She was convinced there had to be an easier way to get around. She had this perfect vision of how things would change in that regard. She said the day would come when people would leave their house, put on a coat, and in this coat, they would have a pad, sort of like a remote control, and on this pad, there would be numbers. Every destination would have an associated code, she explained, and whenever someone wanted to go a particular location, all they would have to do is type the code into the pad and off up into the air they would go. The coat would be the vehicle. They would be transported to the exact location they had typed into the pad. Unlike the process of driving a car, the coat would take them to where they wanted to go without them having to do anything as far as the transporting side of things was concerned. Well, we don't have the coat just yet, but we do have driverless cars so she was right about a vehicle that would take someone to a location without them having to do anything other than type in the location. We also have Eircodes, so she was on the ball about each destination having its own code too. As for the pad, well don't we have satnavs and Google Maps nowadays? Listening to her story back then, it sounded like something you would read in a sci-fi novel.

No matter how many times my mother would tell me that story, I would always ask the same question: when you're up in the air moving along, what would stop you colliding with other people up there? She would explain that there would be a guidance system that would pick up on the fact that there was something in your path. Once it detected the obstacle, it would automatically move you out of the way so as to avoid any potential collision. Again she was right! That technology is available nowadays; sure doesn't almost every car have sensors installed? My mother had the imagination to envision this technology being developed back in a time when a phone or a television was considered the height of all mod cons! There was no internet back then, nothing to influence her thinking. Everything she imagined happening came from within that great mind of hers. I do think she will be proved right about there being a point at which people will start to use the sky above them to make their way around as casually as they would a road or a bike lane.

When it comes to life, we need to always remember that everything is not now as it was before, but everything will not be in the future as it is now either. The only thing we're sure of is that nothing stays the same. Look at how much the world has changed in recent years, and all because of one device, the mobile phone. The big question, however, is: what's next? What will be the next thing to change people's lives?

Well, I believe that 'thing' will be transport. I do wonder, however, with the way things are going, exactly just how far away we are from being able to step out of our houses, punch in a code and head up into the air via some individual platform and be taken straight to our destination. In the future, I think there'll be as many people in the sky above us as there are on the road alongside us. But sure doesn't it make sense? There we are sitting in traffic on the Headford Road in Galway or going mad at the congestion on the Red Cow roundabout above in Dublin, when up above us is a pile of wasted space, just waiting to be used. Wait and you will see, in the years to come, things will go the way I have just described, and you'll be saying to yourself, 'Well, you know, maybe he wasn't raving after all!'

All Roads Lead to Kilgarvan

Now, I'm not a man who indulges in untruths. It's why whenever I'm to be interviewed for live television or otherwise, I will always refuse an offer to see the questions in advance. The way I see it, if you only ever answer truthfully, then what need have you in preparing the answers in the first place?

Sometimes, however, there is an exception to this rule.

Sometimes, a small fib is no harm when it's for the greater good.

Sometimes, it might even be necessary.

A few years back, I was in attendance at the annual Kilgarvan Show. The weather that same day was not good. This show is always a big event for the area, and every year, our mighty organising committee put Trojan effort into making sure the attendees have a great day. In the run-up to the event, however, the biggest worry you'd always have is that the weather wouldn't hold up for the big day in question.

Well, this one particular year, it didn't hold up. In fact, I'd say there was record rainfall all over the county. The one thing that worried me that day was that the weather would stop people coming to the show. You see, the event needs to bring in a certain amount of people each year in order to make the whole thing worthwhile. It isn't about profit or anything like that. The committee just needs to make enough to cover the expenses and to keep the tradition of the show going year after year. This event has been taking place since 1984, so as you can imagine, it has become a big deal for the area.

That day anyway, Radio Kerry was there doing an outside broadcast live from the event. After the show had kicked off, they asked me if I would go on and say a few words. Well sure this was the perfect opportunity to encourage people to come out to the show, so what did I do only go on air and say, 'The weather is bad everywhere in Kerry today, everywhere! But the one place where the sun is shining is in Kilgarvan. We're having a great day here. All roads lead to Kilgarvan and ye'll have a great day when ye come here.'

Now, the power of Radio Kerry is unbelievable. You couldn't imagine a Kerry without Radio Kerry. Whether it's for the deaths, the news or the shows, it's one of those things that if you didn't listen in, you'd feel as though you were missing out on something. Radio Kerry is revered throughout the county, and I'll put it to you this way, if you heard someone on Radio Kerry saying the weather was good in a certain place, such is the influence of the station, you'd be inclined to believe them. Sure enough, people made their way to Kilgarvan, but the big talk when they got there was, 'When did the weather change?'

I was meeting as many as I could throughout the day, so when the topic of the weather was broached by some of the new attendees, all I could do was laugh it off and say, 'Arah God d'you know what, 'twas a great day all along but 'tis after having changed a bit there in the past while!'

That year, despite the weather, the crowd was there, and sure the show's future was sealed for another year. Like I said, a small fib now and then is no harm if it's for the greater good!

Too Far East is West

My attitude in life is simple. It's OK to drink, but not to drink too much. It's OK maybe to have a cigarette now and then, but sure don't be going mad on the things. It's OK to exercise, sure exercise is mighty, but too much exercise can do harm to your body. Don't get me wrong, it's great to take on physical challenges and to push yourself as much as you can, but I do think too much physical pressure on the body can only be a bad thing. We only have little bones, little ankles, little knees and little hips … they can only take so much before they decide, 'Arah look here, I've had enough of this craic!' and sure once that happens, you're rightly goosed!

Likewise, it's OK to take it easy but if you're taking it too easy, you're not helping your body or your health in any way, shape or form.

The moral of the story is that extremes of anything are not good. It's all about moderation.

'Too far east is west,' has always been my belief in life. Don't be going too far east or you'll end up going in the opposite direction altogether. I'm telling you now, that line of advice can be applied to any area of life. Whenever I speak with people of a good age, people like my 104-year-old friend Michael O'Connor, I always make a point of asking them what the secret to a long life is. The response I always get is: 'Everything in moderation. Moderation is everything.'

Now, that vein of thought may be my belief, and I'll stand by it 100%, but I'll be the first to admit that I don't necessarily follow it. When it comes to work, I am a bit extreme. I'd never so much as turn off the phone, because I would be conscious that the one time I do might be the one time someone is in desperate trouble and needs my help. I should listen to my own advice, but I don't, and what's more, I know I won't!

I Think We'd Better Stop, the Door Has Fallen Off

I would honestly say that some of the funniest things that have happened to me happened back when I was either on my way to work or coming from it. Years back, myself and my neighbour Cathal O'Sullivan were driving back from a job in Sneem after having been on diggers for the day. We were in my car, which to be honest wasn't in great shape at the time. Whatever way I took the bend on the road, didn't we hear a bit of a bang. Straight away I looked to my left. Well Cathal was still in the passenger seat alright but there was one thing missing – the door beside him!

Cathal looked at me and got into a fit of laughing. 'I think we'd better stop; the door has fallen off!'

I pulled in, opened the boot of the car and took out some baler twine. Baler twine, for those who don't know, is the twine that holds a bale of hay together. After we retrieved the door, Cathal held it up against the passenger side, right in the place where it had come off, while I got to work with the twine. I swear to God you should never underestimate the power of a couple of winds of bailer twine. We tied the door onto the grab handle on the ceiling before using more twine to then further fasten it in place by attaching it to the passenger seat. It was so secure that by the time we were finished, we were convinced it was as good as when it had come out of the factory. Neither God nor man would have been capable of moving that door from the car again!

There was only one problem. Whenever someone wanted to sit into the passenger seat, they had to either go in the back door and climb out into the front or go in through the driver's side and climb over into the passenger seat. That car I kept for two years after that and every passenger I carried had to climb their way into the seat. If you wanted a lift in my car, by God you worked for your place!

While I was writing the story above, didn't another incident come to mind. This one happened a few years back, when myself and my good friend Dan Casey were working in the forestry supplying timber to Grainger Sawmills. We were working in a place called Mangerton, which was a fine place at the best of times, but during winter, if it snowed, it was near impossible to reach as the closer you got to the forestry, the heavier the snowfall would be. Early one winter's morning, myself and Dan hit off for Mangerton. It had snowed the night before, but to make matters worse, a thick film of frost had developed over the snow, which of course made for atrocious driving conditions. The two of us were in an old Ford Capri car. The Capri was a grand car, nothing to look at and in no great shape, but it got us from A to B and we were damn glad of it. We were a bit worried driving it in the snow, but we were determined to get to work so we carried on nice and slow.

Everything was going fine until we hit the final furlong of the journey to the forestry. The wheels of the car started spinning; the collection of snow and the frost from the night before had become too heavy to drive through. The old Capri, as grand a car as it was, would not be going any further, so we decided it was time to abandon ship and improvise.

We spotted a couple of large fishing tackle boxes in the back of the car. Next we found some spare oil clothes and a bit of rope in the boot. After emptying the boxes of their contents, we took out our chainsaws along with some other pieces of equipment that we needed for the day, including our lunches and, most important, our flasks of tea, and we put the lot into our respective fishing boxes. We then placed the boxes on the ground, and each tied a rope on to the side handle before then wrapping the rope around our waists. There was about a mile of a walk to the forestry so off we headed, dragging the boxes behind us; the same kind of carry-on as the lads over in the Antarctic. We were only in Kilgarvan but if you saw us at dawn that morning with snow stuck in our caps, icicles hanging from our noses and lugging these boxes behind us as we tried to make our way through the snow and into the forest, well mother of God, you'd almost swear it was Lapland we were in! As much as I give out about Dublin, at least when it snows up there, I don't have to resort to tying a box of files to my waist as I try to make my way to Kildare Street.

Dirty Rotten Gobstoppers

There are few things that can quieten a Kerryman, but a gobstopper is one that can, and did, silence this particular Kerryman. Gobstoppers, as you know, are those large round balls of hard sugar sweets that have gum in the centre of them. Horrible dirty things they are, but sure when you're a child, being given a gobstopper was like being given a ball of gold. They were the big thing at the time; everyone absolutely loved them, myself included. One day though, that little love affair quickly fizzled out!

My mother was driving through Kilgarvan village in her Mark 1 Escort; I was around six years of age at the time and sitting in the front passenger seat. As we were passing the Bantry Cross, another car was coming up from it. The woman driving this other car only went and pressed her foot on the accelerator instead of the brake. Sure didn't she go flying right across the road and straight into the side of my mother's car. The force of the collision was such that I remember thinking we were going to be driven in through the door of Mrs Shine's shop nearby. Mother of God, the belt was something else.

Now I firmly believe that cars were stronger back then, so my mother's car was able for the impact, but you have to remember that the other car involved was also very strong, so the force of the smash jolted us from our seats. As bad luck would have it, I had been sucking on a gobstopper at the point of impact, but rather than fall out of my mouth, didn't the dirty rotten thing only go and roll in the opposite direction – back down my throat. It wouldn't have been so bad if the gobstopper had been sucked down to a smaller size at that point, but this one was nearly the size of my mouth, so naturally, when it went back, it lodged in my throat. Straight away, I got my mother's attention and gestured at my throat. She looked at me for a second but wasn't long realising from the panic on my face what was after happening. Quickly she hit me a belt on my back and out came the gobstopper.

Not once since that day have I been able to so much as look at a gobstopper. You could have offered me a lorry load of them, and I'd say I'd have been sick on the spot at the thought of going near even just one. I swear to God, there's nothing like a bit of trauma to put you off the sweet stuff! When I think back on it now, I can't understand how the size of them didn't wipe out kids on all sides back then. Sure they were lethal! They weren't sweets at all, more like choke bombs, to be honest.

Windscreens and Smithereens

There was a lifelong friend of my parents called Jack Grady, and Jack, God rest his soul, was a great man for dealing in motor cars, lorries, repairs and parts. He had a garage on the Park Road in Killarney and when I was a young lad, I remember him always being the go-to man for car repairs and car purchases. My mother used to always buy her car from Jack, and that was where she bought her Mark 1 Escort. Now, sometimes you could buy a nice fine car, but for whatever reason, it would just be the most troublesome divil of a thing. Well this Mark 1 Escort was exactly that. From the day my mother bought it, it was always giving her trouble. It must have been a Monday morning car.

Every time it would give her grief, she would head back to Jack with it. The car would splutter its way into Jack's yard, and there she would leave it until he got it going again. One day, however, when my mother and I went back to Jack's yard to collect the car, we spotted a beautiful new car as we were walking in. Well, it was as shiny! We even both remarked on how well it looked. My mother approached Jack and asked if her car was ready.

'It is! I have it down the yard there,' said Jack. 'Sure lookit, it's an auld troublesome car, nothing but this and that wrong with it, but I have a nice car out the front there and I took your stuff out of the old car and put them into that one.'

Sure enough, he was talking about the beautiful shiny car we had just been admiring.

'Oh my God, Jack, that's very nice of you, but how much is that car?' my mother asked.

'Look, it cost me a bit extra but you're such a nice woman and so easygoing about the fact that I sold you a car that has caused you nothing but trouble. In fairness to you, you never got cross, or even opened your mouth about it, so it's only right that I give you this car.'

My mother was shocked.

'Jack, you can't afford to do that!'

'No, I have my mind made up and nothing will make me change it,' he said back to her.

Now that was an example of Jack Grady's generosity of spirit. He was the nicest man you could meet, but there was the other tough side to him, and my God, that was a side that you would meet at your own peril. I remember one famous day when a right piece of work walked into Jack's yard. Now this lad was known to be a bit of a smartalec; he wasn't one bit liked around the place. Sure as soon as he walked in, Jack was sizing him up. He knew this lad was going to be an awkward one. The man approached Jack and told him he was looking to buy a windscreen. At that time, if you broke a windscreen, you'd have to look for a second-hand replacement. There was certainly no company to come out and fix the screen for you. You had to go to a scrap yard, buy a windscreen from an older car and then have it fitted into your car. Anyway, Jack brought the man over to the corner of the yard where there was a fine replacement and in perfect condition too. Right from the start, however, this man had taken an attitude with Jack, and Jack's patience with him was starting to run a little thin.

'How much do you want for it, Jack?' he asked.

'Five pound,' he replied.

'Arah sure look, if I give you two pound, won't it be plenty for it?'

Jack looked at the man. 'Is it two pound you'll offer me?' he asked.

'Not only will I offer you two pound, I won't give you a penny more!' said the man back to him.

Well that put the tin hat on things. Jack kept his cool, and quickly scanned the ground before setting his eyes on an iron bar.

He grabbed the bar and without any hesitation, drew an all-merciful belt on the windscreen. Well the windscreen shattered into a thousand bits and pieces. Jack looked at the man, who was now shell-shocked, got into a fit of laughing and said, 'I'll tell you what you can do! You can pick up the windscreen and take it away for nothing now!'

And with that, Jack threw the bar on the ground, and left the smart-alec standing there in disbelief at the carnage that had just taken place before him. There was no way he was going to get another windscreen to fit his car window in Kerry that day. He knew he had blown his chance with Jack by being too smart with him. It's like the skinning of the cat. There's a hundred ways to do it and there was a hundred ways in which that man could have approached Jack. Instead, he made a complete bags of it, and in doing so, burned his bridge with the one man who had what he wanted.

Jack was a dealing man, you see; if the man had just negotiated with him, it was likely Jack would have brought the price down. Granted, by smashing a perfectly good windscreen, Jack had left himself out of pocket and without a windscreen to sell, but you know something, I'd say the value of satisfaction he got from putting the county smartarse in his place was probably worth a lot more than five pound!

Something to Remember Me By

A few days before my mother passed away, I brought her for a drive back to beautiful Slea Head to see the scenery. During our trip, we stopped off at the showroom of Louis Mulcahy, the famous potter. No sooner were we in the door when she was insisting on buying some little bits and pieces for the group of us who were there. Sure I didn't want her to buy me anything, but do you think she would listen? Not a hope! She went and bought everyone a little something. In hindsight I realised there was a significance in what she was doing. She knew she hadn't long left and that these little gifts would be the last thing she would give each of us.

Off she went to see Louis Mulcahy's displays and back she came with a little box for me. What had she bought for me but a fine mug. She knew exactly what she was doing when she bought that particular item for me. You see, I'm a fright for minding things, and if I'm given something sentimental, it could even be a biro, well you could be sure I would mind it. She knew I wouldn't just mind the mug, I'd treasure it.

Now, if I'm having a cup of tea in the house, I always make sure to use the mug my mother bought me. Sure she knew only too well that I would do that. Every time I'm drinking my cup of tea now, I always think of her. I think of the nice fine day we had back in Slea Head, and I remember every minute of our trip out there together. It was her way of giving me a little something to remember her by – and her intention worked out to a T.

What Comes Before You Now ...

Every time I drive through the village of Inch, I always think back to the last time I brought my mother there. It was during her final few days in this world. We had spent some time looking out at the beach, and then afterwards, I carried her from the car to Sammy's Café, where we had a bite to eat. While we were sitting in the café, she was looking up at a nearby guesthouse that was overlooking the beach. The house was actually owned by Sammy, the owner of the café. Well, my mother thought this house looked the picture of beauty, so I suggested to her that we get into the car and head on up to it for a look.

Sure enough, we went up to the house and I knocked on the door. When a lovely woman answered, I explained how my mother had been admiring the house and was wondering what the view of the beach would be like from the window. They invited us in, and very kindly arranged chairs for us so we could sit in the living room and admire the view in comfort. We spent around twenty minutes chatting while looking out at the beautiful landscape. My mother was enthralled by it.

'Do you know what we'll do one of the days?' I said to her. 'We'll come back here and stay a night or two, and you can look out the window again.'

She was delighted by the idea and agreed we would do it.

Unfortunately, it was within the following seven or eight days that she left us. There was no chance of us coming back to enjoy the view again. If you take one thing from this book, let it be this: when you have a chance, seize it, because you might never get it again. What comes before you now might not come before you again.

The Final Resting Place

My mother knew exactly where she wanted to be buried. Aghadoe graveyard. We were so lucky to get a plot there as you actually can't get one there these days unless you already own an existing plot. When my mother was sick, and we knew her time on this earth was limited, we still couldn't buy the plot there. The popularity and demand for this particular graveyard was such that a plot could not be purchased until the person was deceased.

There's actually a wonderful viewing area across the road from the graveyard in the Aghadoe Heights Hotel, and the week before my mother passed, I brought her there to look out at the lake and the landscape. I will never forget how happy she was to be there, so as painful as it was to subsequently lose her, there's at least some solace to be found from the fact that her final resting place is in the one area she loved so much.

That plot in Aghadoe graveyard is where I'll be buried as well. I've already discussed it with my family and told them what I want. I think everyone should talk about their final wishes with those closest to them. I don't think families should make the decision as to where a loved one should be buried. I think the only person who should decide is the person who is going to be buried. In fairness, 'tis yourself who will be going in there and not anyone else, so you might as well do your future late self a favour and ensure it's somewhere you like. Even if you're in the best of health, for God's sake put your burial wishes in writing.

I know it sounds extreme, but there's a lot to be said for buying a plot. It has happened on a number of occasions in Killarney and other areas in Kerry where graves were so scarce, people were faced with the proposition of being buried in other places. I'll never forget the article in *The Kerryman* which explicitly stated that 'people were not going to cross the river to Knocknagree to be buried'. The very notion of a person from Kerry being buried in Cork had people riled up altogether.

I don't know if it's like this in other countries, but in rural Ireland, a final resting place is extremely important to a person. More so than you'd realise. So too, of course, is the funeral itself. This is where rural Ireland really gets it right. We know how to give our loved ones a mighty send-off. Sure some of the wakes I've been at have been as good as, if not better, than some weddings. In fact, there's a great saying that a good funeral in Kilgarvan is way better than a bad wedding in Kenmare!

I believe Kerry is especially blessed with some of the finest undertakers you could hope to have oversee your send-off. The reason for their quality of work, shall we say, is because they are of long standing. I know of undertakers who would actually be third and fourth generation. One undertaker even married a lovely woman who was actually the daughter of another undertaker!

Not everyone is capable of dealing with people when they're at their most vulnerable, but the undertakers I know all have a great understanding of that. Then there are elements of the business that would be 'unwritten', so to speak; just certain rules that they would have learned from the generations that went before them. One particular Kerry undertaker abides by the 'age rule', in that if a young person under a certain age passes away, there is no bill for the funeral. That was an old rule at one time in Kerry, and some undertakers still adhere to it. Death is always difficult, but the sudden passing of someone very young is especially hard to deal with, so the age rule was employed.

I have seen remarkable care, diligence and understanding from undertakers. Their diplomatic skills are absolutely brilliant because they would have to defuse situations that might arise between family members when tensions are running high. They are constantly having to deal with people who are tired, grieving and possibly in a state of shock. I used to say the diplomacy of undertakers made them almost like politicians, but you know, the more I think about the level of empathy and support an undertaker offers, the more I'm starting to think 'tis the politicians who could learn a thing or two from the undertakers.

Rituals

It's a terribly morbid thing to say, but all the old Irish rituals that surrounded a person's death, well, they're actually awful interesting when you look into them. I can still remember various customs that would be carried out whenever a passing would occur; a good few of them are still implemented to this day. For instance, when there was a death in the house, a window would be opened to allow the spirit of the deceased to leave, but the most important thing of all about this particular ritual was that no one could stand in the path of the open window. If you stopped the spirit leaving, there was a belief that you would go on to endure many a misfortune in life.

Another ritual that was always adhered to was the stopping of the clock in the room where the death had occurred. Sometimes, all the clocks in the house would be stopped. The mirrors were also covered with a towel or else turned around to face the wall. If mirrors were not shrouded, especially in the room where the passing had taken place, there was the belief that the soul of the deceased might become trapped in the mirror.

When you think about it, these traditions might sound outlandish in the light of today's culture, but these rituals and beliefs were taken so seriously at one time, not to mention adhered to with military-style precision. I'd honestly hate to see any of these practices being abandoned or forgotten about. Some might consider them a relic from times past, but I do believe the loss of those customs would be the loss of an awful important element of Irish culture.

Jackie x 2

My father was always adamant that the only person who could take him off was Donal Twomey. Donal had an unbelievable talent for impersonating him; he'd mimic his voice and mannerisms to a T. The other person who came close was Dermot Morgan.

When my father was on *The Late Late Show* one night, afterwards myself and my wife, Eileen, headed back to the hotel to meet him in the bar for a drink. As we were sitting in the bar, who do you think should walk in the door only Fr Ted himself, Dermot Morgan! It turns out he had been at home watching my father on the *Late Late* when he decided he'd head out to his local for a pint. As soon as he spotted us, over he came. Straight away he said, 'Lads close yer eyes!' We did as we were asked. Next thing, Dermot started impersonating my father and what he had said on the *Late Late*. You'd swear to God you were listening to a recording of my father's interview. Dermot was an expert at it; a genuinely gifted mimic. Even more impressive is that Dermot was impersonating him solely from the memory of what he had heard my father say about an hour beforehand on the show. He had no idea he was going to end up bumping into us later that night. He had been heading out for a pint not realising we were in the same place he was going to. We had never met him before that night so we didn't know each other, but we ended up having a great chat and promised we would meet up again. I swear to God, a couple of weeks later didn't I hear the news that he had passed away. I got an awful land when I heard. He was taken way too soon.

Another gifted comic and actor whom we lost far too soon was the beloved Brendan Grace. I always enjoyed Brendan's comedy and found him to be so genuine and warm. We used to love it when Brendan would take off my father as part of his routine. My father got mileage out of it. About two months after my father passed away, Brendan phoned me. He very kindly asked if I would mind him continuing to feature the Jackie Healy-Rae character in his shows. Straight away I told him I was speaking with the authority of my father when I said he could. My father was always a believer in the idea that people should keep moving and keep going regardless, and so I felt it would be an awful thing for Brendan to go silent on him. I told him if he could put people laughing by featuring my father in his act, then both I and the family would only be delighted to see that continue.

Whether you were eight years of age or eighty, you could go to a Brendan Grace gig and enjoy every bit of it. The reason for this, I believe, goes back to a talk he'd had with Mrs Margaret O'Donoghue, who owned Killarney's Gleneagle Hotel and INEC along with her husband, Maurice. She relayed to me a story about when Brendan was first starting out as a young entertainer.

He performed in the Gleneagle one night, and after his show, Mrs O'Donoghue called him to one side for a word. She told him that he could have a great career in singing and in comedy but that the one thing he should do to keep his audience wide and large was to keep his jokes as clean as possible. He took her advice on board and if you ever studied his routine, you'd notice that regardless of what he was joking about, he would never cross the line.

The really intelligent thing about Brendan's act was that it wasn't just what he said that made people laugh, it was what he didn't say! That's what would really put you laughing. When he'd perform his Father of the Bride routine, his mannerisms alone would have you howling with laughter. A lot of comedians seem to think that when they get up on stage, they have to start effing and blinding and insulting people, but the best never resort to that. I honestly believe the secret of Brendan's success lay in that talk he'd had with Mrs O'Donoghue all those years ago. Her friendly advice resonated with him and he never strayed from it during his career.

When we heard the news of Brendan's illness, we were all very shocked and worried for him. I had kept in contact with him and his family, and on the Wednesday morning before he passed away, he and I enjoyed a chat over the phone. He was asking how everyone was and wanted to know what was happening in Kerry. We also spoke about some mutual friends of ours from Kerry, in particular a number of older people that he had come to know quite well.

During that call, he also referenced a letter I had written to him just a few days earlier. In that last conversation, he recalled the contents of the letter, which were very personal to me and of course to Brendan. What I will say, however, is that the letter reflected what I felt the people of Kerry and Ireland thought of him. I also emphasised how proud we were of him and how much we appreciated the laughs and entertainment he had given us over the years. He jokingly told me, in the way only Brendan could, that not only had he read the letter, but that he was still reading it and was going to keep on reading it.

When word of Brendan's passing filtered through social media the following night, a profound sadness was evident in people's reactions. The turnout for his funeral the following Monday said it all. I thought his manager, Brian Keane, gave an exceptionally wonderful speech. I don't know Brian well, but I had met him a few times before the funeral. Sometimes in life you'd know a nice person by looking at them. If Brendan liked someone, you'd know they were the salt of the earth. Brian told a lovely story up on the altar about how he first came to meet Brendan. He was sixteen years of age and working in his father's petrol station in an area of Dublin where Brendan was living. One night Brendan pulled into the petrol station in his Jaguar and asked the young Brian to fill the tank. Brian dutifully did as he was asked and when the tank was full, Brendan turned and said to him, 'Will you fill up the other one as well?' Jaguar cars have two tanks, which Brian hadn't been aware of until that point, so of course with Brian being a young lad, he found himself awful impressed by this big car with its two tanks and the lovely man driving it. Brendan became a regular customer at the petrol station, but Brian had convinced himself that he was coming in because he enjoyed talking to him. He wasn't far wrong. It wasn't too long before Brendan approached Brian and asked him to come working for him. At the time, Brian was being paid forty pound a week to work for his father, which he was very happy to do, but when he was working for Brendan, well, the days were just as long but he was getting thirty pound a day, which back then was an absolute pile of money, especially for a teenager. Brian went on to become Brendan's roadie, his organiser, his manager, the chief cook and bottle washer of the whole show. And to think it all started from a chance meeting in a petrol station!

That day in the church, as we listened to Brian's speech, what struck me was how heartfelt, funny, and poignant it was. It was everything that a speech would be when given by someone who genuinely cared. He also kept the congregation entertained by recalling how, in the final days, Brendan jokingly told him to be sure to have a big crowd at the funeral so they could set up a merchandise stall at the end of the church and shift some of the last of the DVDs and CDs. In true BG style, he also instructed Brian to 'cut the priest in for 20%'. Fr Brian D'Arcy, who was officiating, got a great kick out of that!

Even at his own funeral, Brendan was making people laugh. During his career, he didn't just entertain, he also created many memories for people. Never was this more evident than after his passing when everyone's Facebook newsfeeds were filled with people sharing not only their photos with him but also their stories from their encounters with him. After all, whenever Brendan came off the stage, he never went out the back door, he would always head straight into the crowd to meet the people who had paid to see him that night. He would stand and sign autographs for as long as was required, and sure once everyone had a camera phone, well it's no exaggeration to say that he would also stand and smile for over a thousand photos on any given night. He didn't go through the motions either; everyone who met him got to meet the lively entertainer they were expecting. He always made time for fans after his shows because he knew he belonged to the people. That was the thing about Brendan. He belonged to everybody, and absolutely everybody loved him for it.

The Last One Standing

A very good friend of mine, Maurice 'Mottie' O'Donoghue, was one of those people who was full of kind gestures. He was just the most genuine type of person you could hope to meet. I remember when he went into the oil business, he became a distributor for Top Oil in Glenflesk, which is between Killarney and Kilgarvan. Given his popularity, his larger-than-life character, and his partiality for good craic, well, needless to say, his business did brilliantly, and it wasn't long before he had built up a loyal customer base. In fact, he ended up becoming a very big supplier of oil in a very short space of time. One day, Maurice Mottie's Top Oil boss, the former Cork hurler Justin McCarthy, called out to his house where he lived with his mother Peggie.

Now, Maurice Mottie had these lovely green fields which were up on a height, so Justin asked if they could head up for a walk as he wanted to see the view from above. Off they went and when they got to the top, they took a break for a few minutes and sat on a big stone in the middle of the field. The stone they were sitting on was like something that had been sculpted by God himself. It was one of those rocks that was naturally smooth and shaped like a seat. There they were, anyway, looking down over the lakes of Killarney, and taking in the beautiful view, when Justin happened to make a passing remark about their unusual seat, saying something along the lines of, 'Well do you know something, I'd love to have a stone like this in my own garden.'

A couple of weeks later, Justin was in his office over in Cork when he got a phone call. It was Maurice Mottie calling from a payphone.

'Where are you?' he asked.

'I'm here at work,' said Justin.

'Well, look, you'd better come out to your house right away.'

'Why? What's wrong with my house?'

'Arah, I've a little thing there for you ...' Maurice Mottie explained. 'Sure maybe you might come out to the house for a minute?'

Well Justin was bamboozled, bewildered, bemused, all the Bs, as to what Maurice Mottie wanted him for, so out he went to the house to see what was going on. What do you think Maurice Mottie was after doing? He was after going to the awful trouble of digging the stone out of the field. He then got his tractor and trailer and transported the stone from the field down to the edge of the road, where he loaded it into his lorry. Next he headed for Cork with the stone inside in the back of the lorry. He had hired a digger to take the stone out of the lorry when he arrived in Cork, but what he wanted Justin for was to find out exactly where in the garden he wanted the digger to place the stone. Justin of course was absolutely gobsmacked by this. The stone was set in place and sure Justin was delighted with his new feature. It was the talk of the city that he'd had a stone delivered from Kerry to his garden in Cork!

That was Maurice Mottie to a T. Always going above and beyond for people.

In February of 1990, I was involved in a very serious road accident which left me in a full body cast, not to mention in need of walking aids for years that followed. I wrote about the accident in the last book, and I'll be honest, I've had a long hard day and I'm in no mood to go recalling the ins and outs of it all again! While I was in hospital, however, Maurice Mottie and another very good friend of ours, a building contractor, John O'Connor, called in to see me very regularly. The three of us were very good friends, and with us being in our twenties, we would have often had the craic and gone places together. We also worked together on various jobs as well, so you could say we were in and out of each other's lives very frequently.

That following September, anyway, myself and my father were inside in Maurice Mottie's yard. He'd had a small problem he· wanted our help with, so he wrote down some details on a sheet of paper and handed it to my father, who in turn put it in his inside pocket. We said our goodbyes and headed off for Limerick. Maurice Mottie meanwhile sat into his jeep and took off to Cork, where he had a job on. By the time my father would take the note out from his inside pocket that night, Maurice Mottie would be dead. He had been involved in a fatal road accident while making his way to Cork that morning. I remember his Top Oil boss, Justin McCarthy, told me afterwards that every time he drew the curtains in the morning, he would see the famous stone and immediately his face would break into a smile as the first person who would come into his mind would be Maurice Mottie.

By the end of that same year, a car accident had also claimed the life of John O'Connor. On the night of his removal, I went to pay my respects to the family. I was still in a bad shape after my own accident earlier that year, but looking back, my head wasn't in a great way either after having lost two very good friends in the space of a couple of months. I'll never forget John's poor father catching my hand. 'Out of the three of ye,' he said, 'you're the last one left standing.'

You're the last one left standing.

Never in all my life will I forget the impact of those six words, and the sorrow and anguish they instantly struck me with.

We'll Leave It Here So

If I ever die, and that's a big if, the one thing I'd like is for people to enjoy themselves at the funeral. I believe that a funeral should be a celebration of a life and not the mourning of a death. Obviously, where there's a tragedy or a sudden passing, well, you can't have celebration per se because the feeling is one of shock, but if a person has lived to a good age and enjoyed a long life, well then you should be celebrating that person's life when they pass on to what I believe is an eternal reward. Some people think you go into a hole and that's the end of it. I don't choose to believe that. I believe that there is a heaven and a hell, and if my time to depart should arrive, well, I would obviously be hoping to be going up rather than down if at all possible. Before I go, though, there's a medal I'd like to try and get. Unusually, for a Kerry man, the medal I've set my sights on isn't of the GAA All-Ireland variety. No, the one I want is the birthday medal. Let me explain further.

When you reach the age of 100, you receive a congratulatory letter from the president and a Centenarian Bounty consisting of a cheque for €2,540. A lot of people don't realise you get a cheque when your age hits three digits, but even more are unaware that you get a commemorative medal when you turn 101. In fact, Áras an Uachtaráin sends you a medal for every birthday you live through after that. These medals are a very precious memento as they are an acknowledgement of reaching such a milestone. I remember on one occasion, I got a very unusual request from a family in which there were four siblings. Their mother had received a medal from her 101st birthday onwards, but had passed away just a few days shy of her 104th birthday and so she didn't receive the fourth medal. Each sibling had been given one of the medals as a memento. However, because the mother had received three, it meant there was one sibling left without. The family were upset by this and so they contacted me to see if I could get on to Áras an Uachtaráin and ask if there was any hope of still getting the medal for the deceased as they had passed away only a few days before their birthday. I did as I was asked. Unfortunately, the response I got from Áras an Uachtaráin was that this was one of the most common requests they received and so they had to become extremely strict on the matter. Their rule was simple. Unless you lived through the day of the birthday in question, you would not receive the medal. Given the criteria involved in being able to secure one of these medals, their rarity has made them almost like a collector's item.

The one thing I certainly won't get a medal for is the amount of time I spend at home. The job of a TD is not of the nine to five variety by any means. There are days when you would go in the door of your home, change your clothes, grab a sandwich while on the phone and be gone out the door again. Then there could be days on end where you might not be home at all. I'm very lucky to have such a very understanding wife in Eileen. Most people would say to their other halves, 'let's go for a drive', or 'let's go for a drink'. I'd like to be able to say we do that, but the truth of the matter is that I never have time to do those things. It doesn't matter if there's an election on or not, the fact is, there's always something on. I'll never try to make myself out to be something that I'm not. I have always been one for admitting my faults, and I have to say not dedicating time to my own family is certainly one of them.

I always hear of people being described as a family person, or as someone who always put their family first, and that's a wonderful thing to be able to say about an individual, but unfortunately that is not something that somebody would be able to say about me. If a person was to tell the truth about me, what they'd say is, 'Well he loved his family dearly, but in the end, he always put the job, his constituents and the county of Kerry first.' There has often been a situation whereby I would have great intentions of going to some family event at 9pm on a Friday evening. If I received a call, however, telling me there was a deputation that wanted to meet at that same time, or if there was a constituent in need of assistance, well I won't deny for one second that I would go to where the deputation, the constituent, or whoever it may be, wanted to meet me. If I were to give you the impression of anything else, I wouldn't be honest.

The notion of retirement terrifies me, and what's even more terrifying is that I don't decide when I retire, the people do. The idea of not being busy is an awful frightening notion, though. From the second I get up in the morning, my brain is always in work mode, thinking about a constituent's problem or a task that I might have to carry out for someone. I couldn't imagine what retirement would be like but, please God, with the support of the public, it hopefully won't be a fear I'll have to face for some time yet.

On average, a person will see 30,000 mornings. Don't waste one of them.

— MHR